Whose games have been viewed more than 17 million times on YouTube?

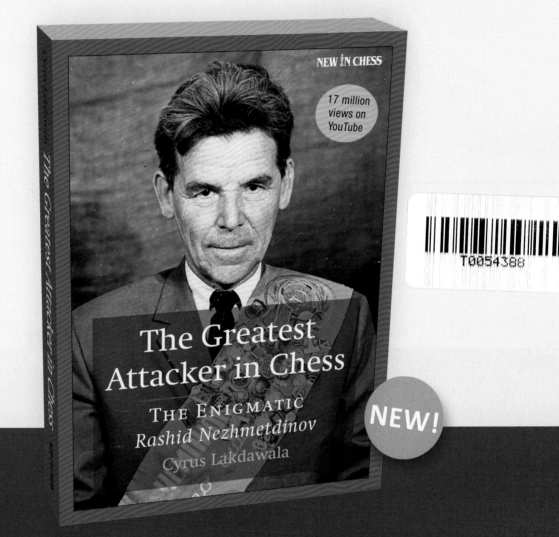

paperback | 288 pages | €29.95 | available at your local (chess)bookseller or at newinchess.com | a NEW IN CHESS publication

Winning the World Open
is as entertaining as it is instructive

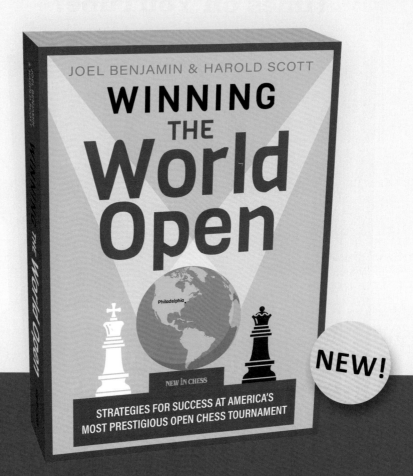

JOEL BENJAMIN & HAROLD SCOTT

WINNING THE World Open

Philadelphia

NEW IN CHESS

STRATEGIES FOR SUCCESS AT AMERICA'S MOST PRESTIGIOUS OPEN CHESS TOURNAMENT

NEW!

For nearly fifty years, grandmasters and amateurs alike have been making their annual pilgrimage to the World Open, an iconic event in American chess with large entry fees and large prizes. Every year around the 4th of July, Philadelphia is the scene of countless epic battles at the board.

Two-time winner and GM Joel Benjamin and chess columnist Harold Scott examined hundreds of games and conducted a series of interviews with what they call the Heroes of the World Open, players who won the tournament on multiple occasions.

What they wanted to know: why have some players been so consistent in their efforts, always battling for the top prizes? Benjamin and Scott discovered that the Heroes definitely had one common factor: their fighting spirit!

The authors present the history of the World Open, from its humble beginnings to the juggernaut it has become today. *Winning the World Open* is as entertaining as it is instructive.

paperback | 344 pages | €29.95 | available at your local (chess)bookseller or at newinchess.com | a **NEW IN CHESS** publication

'Chess players don't need to find a hobby when they retire.'

6 Moscow Metro
The coming months a 'Chess Train' will run on the Sokolnicheskaya line, the oldest in the metro of the Russian capital.

8 NIC's Café
An 'extremely rare' chess photo taken in 1863 by Charles Dodgson (better known as Lewis Carroll) will be auctioned at Bonhams in New York.

11 Your Move
What is wrong with Chess960?, GM David Navara wonders.

12 Meltdown in Dubai
The World Championship match in Dubai ended in a shockingly easy victory for Magnus Carlsen. The defending champion only needed 11 games to trounce Ian Nepomniachtchi 7½-3½.

19 Celeb64: Tim Krabbé

24 Fair & Square
'Chess gets a hold of some people, like a virus or a drug.'

32 Match infographic

36 Adult improvement
James Altucher writes about an aspect of the world title match that appeals to all of us: the blunders.

38 The Silicon Road
Matthew Sadler looks at the role engines played in 'the first World Championship match in the era of neural networks'.

44 When Patti met Bobby
How many songs did Patti Smith, the godmother of punk, really sing together with Bobby Fischer when they met in Reykjavik in 2005?

48 Rapid World Championship
All eyes were on the usual suspects, but they all had to bow to Uzbek GM Nodirbek Abdusattorov (17!) .

66 Magnus Carlsen teaches chess
Banter Blitz is fun and instructive, especially if you play the number one player on the planet.

68 MVL World Blitz Champion
Maxime Vachier-Lagrave won his first Blitz world title, as he kept his cool in the tiebreak, dashing the hopes of local favourite Jan-Krzysztof Duda.

78 Maximize Your Tactics
Find the right moves.

80 Judit Polgar
Lessons in perseverance with two brilliant prize-winning studies.

85 What would you play?
Test your decision-making skills with Thomas 'Toolbox' Willemze.

89 They are the Champions
Haritomeni Markantonaki is the national women's champion of Greece.

90 Sadler on Books
The second volume of *Masterpieces and Dramas of the Soviet Championships (1938-1947)* earns warm praise from our book reviewer Matthew Sadler (5 stars!).

96 Euwe to the Max
Jan Timman argues that Max Euwe not only held the world title but that at his peak he was also the strongest player in the world.

106 Just Checking
What is John Donaldson's life motto?

CONTRIBUTORS TO THIS ISSUE
James Altucher, Erwin l'Ami, Magnus Carlsen, Maxim Dlugy, John Donaldson, Jorden van Foreest, Anish Giri, John Henderson, Dylan McClain, Peter Heine Nielsen, Maxim Notkin, Judit Polgar, Matthew Sadler, Han Schut, Jan Timman, Jonathan Tisdall, Thomas Willemze

Moscow Metro Chess Train

On New Year's Eve, a distinctive new train went into service in Moscow, a metro train that will allow its passengers to catch up on their chess history and knowledge.

The train will run on the Sokolnicheskaya line, the oldest in the Moscow metro. The No 32 with its five coaches will chronicle the history of the game, its evolution in the Soviet Union and in Russia, show images of the world's elite players from chess magazines, plus chess in art, theatre, literature and cinema. And all this wrapped in a spectacular black and white chess livery.

On hand for the launch of the underground chess museum on wheels were 12th World Champion Anatoly Karpov, Dmitry Bogachev (producer of *Chess: the Musical* and Artistic Director of the MDM Theatre), Yulia Temnikova (Deputy CEO of Client Services of the Moscow Metro), Mikhail Minin (General Director of MTS Entertainment), and the CFR Chess Museum's curator, Dmitry Oleinikov.

The new chess train's addition to the Moscow Metro is a joint effort from FIDE, the Russian Chess Federation, the Broadway Moscow Theatre Company, and MTS Entertainment. The service will run for six months. ∎

Through the Looking-Glass

In October 1863, Charles Dodgson, better known by his pseudonym Lewis Carroll, visited the Rossetti family in their London home. There, through the glass of his lens, he photographed the poet and painter Dante Gabriel Rossetti playing chess against his mother, Frances Polidori, with poet sister Christina looking on benignly.

Dante Gabriel Rossetti, his poet sister Christina, and chess immortalized by Lewis Carroll. How poetic can a photo be?

Dodgson's 'extremely rare' portrait of the famous pre-Raphaelite literary family – one of only three complete images known in existence – came up for auction in a pre-Christmas Fine Books and Manuscripts sale at Bonhams in New York, attracting a lot of interest as no similar quality original Dodgson photograph of the Rossetti family had sold on the open market in recent years.

The auction house put an estimate of $50,000-70,000 on it. But alas, Dodgson's arranged and printed chess photo of the Rossettis did not find a buyer after failing to reach its reserve price. Bonhams have already informed collectors that it will go back on sale again later in the new year.

Coincidently, around the same time as this photo was taken, Dodgson's *Alice's Adventures in Wonderland* was conceived as a fantasy story adventure for a colleague's young daugh-

ters, and published in 1865. The *Through the Looking-Glass* sequel followed in 1871. The story famously draws on chess imagery, inspired by Dodgson's experiences teaching one of the daughters how to play the game, and widely believed where the chess study/problem term 'fantasy chess' originated from.

Chess in Slums

According to UNICEF, one in every five of the world's out-of-school children in Nigeria and over 80 million Nigerians live in extreme poverty. A recent media feature of one of those slums appeared in *The Sunday Times* offering hope through chess, to ensure that these children have a chance in life. The saviour is Tunde Onakoya.

As a kid from a similar slum, two years out of school and only 10 years old, Tunde Onakoya latched onto the game after watching it being played, and never let go. He returned to school and joined a chess club, won a chess scholarship to college and rose to No 13 in his country. 'Chess literally saved me', said the Nigerian master.

Three years ago, Onakoya decided to 'give back' by also using chess as his tool: taking the game back to the slums to help others find better opportunities. He started small in Lagos, and his charity Chess in Slums Africa expanded with a team

Nigerian master Tunde Onakoya hopes that chess will help the children in slums find a better future.

of like-minded volunteers. Recently, Onakoya announced a major new $1 million partnership with Venture Garden Group, which calls itself Africa's largest tech incubator.

Their goal is to reach a million children through the project within five years – the idea being that those sponsored will not be turned into budding Grandmasters but rather steered towards careers in tech. The initiative also received an added boost with funding and learning materials from ChessKid, the US charity arm of chess.com, and donors have also given an additional £45,000.

Chess Got Talent

Last year, these pages (New In Chess 2021/5) told the tale of the mysterious Spanish chess sensation

Rey Enigma remains a mystery after he escaped with a draw (and had almost won) against Anatoly Karpov.

'Rey Enigma', who keeps his identity a secret by being dressed head to foot in a black and white checkered jumpsuit. He quickly turned into an unlikely media sensation by popping up all over the place and throwing down chess challenges.

His true identity is a closely guarded secret – but he promised to reveal his identity if he lost a game on TV. This led to a special challenge being issued to Rey Enigma to appear in the season-ending December 17 edition of the 'Spain's Got Talent Grand Final 7' to play former World Champion Anatoly Karpov.

After the niceties of a general introduction, the two combatants got down to business by battling it out over a closely-fought 3+0 blitz game that was equal throughout. But the game turned wildly during the vagaries of the time-scramble, as first Enigma missed his moment of glory in front of a huge TV audience in the diagrammed position, with Karpov blundering.

Rey Enigma – Anatoly Karpov
Spain's Got Talent Grand Final 2021

1...♘f4?? 2.♖f3?
Winning on-the-spot was 2.♖e3!, with Black losing a piece.
2...♘e6 3.♕xe5 dxe5 4.♖e3 ♘d4
The position was back to equal again, but both players had little to no time left. The 12th World Champion should have had a clear winning advantage, as Enigma was down to his bare king surrounded by black pieces, only for Karpov's flag to fall and the game being declared a draw... and with it, Rey Enigma's identity still remains a secret!

Black is OK

Back in 1966, Yoko Ono unveiled her artistic take on chess with her White Chess Set. Now comes new wave artist Kim Dacres with her current solo exhibition 'Black Moves First' at GAVLAK Los Angeles gallery in West Palm Beach that aims to disrupt the rules of the game, both in chess and art.

Dacres's installation featured in *Cultured* magazine and stems from her long interest in chess as well as her questioning of its rules. 'Why does White always move first?' the artist rhetorically asks. Looking at the dynamics of the game through

Kim Dacres with her chess pieces. 'I understand that chess is not a game, it's about war.'

the lens of today's social landscape, 'Black folks have to navigate a world where they're not given the priority to make the first move,' she explains.

The show's eight mixed-media sculptures are made of automobile and bicycle tyres in addition to a range of hardware that Dacres assembles at her studio with jigsaw, drills and heavy-duty scissors. Though monochromatic, their varying sheens reveal the chromatic range of the colour black. The eye-level height totems pay homage to matriarchal figures in the artist's family, and personalities are represented in facial expressions and sartorial details.

'As a history buff, I understand that chess is not a game, it's about war,' says the artist. 'Entering any space as a Black queer woman artist is not so different either.'

Going Viral

The World Rapid and Blitz Championships in Warsaw, Poland, was an entertaining way to end the year and promised lots of thrills 'n' spills on the boards. But for one young local hero, a thrilling spill incident went viral and unwittingly thrust him into the limelight.

The player in question was 18-year-old Pole Pawel Teclaf, and it all happened during his Round 10 encounter in the Blitz Championship with Tigran L. Petrosian, just as the latter had made his winning move. Teclaf had set up a fortress but hadn't noticed he had blundered away the draw, and threw himself back in his chair with an hilarious overreaction to falling into a mate-in-two... That moment was soon-to-be shared online, as he's seen flying backwards off his chair and tumbling onto the floor.

It wasn't till the next day that our hero realized through the live video stream and the comical end to his game, that overnight he'd unwittingly turned into an online sensation. 'In the morning,' he explained when interviewed by the FIDE official site, 'I was in the elevator and a person standing next to me was staring at me and on her phone back and forth, smirking. When I go to

Unperturbed, Tigran Petrosian watches as Pawel Teclaf realizes that it's not a fortress at all!

my room, I opened WhatsApp and saw plenty of links and realized I am getting popular.'

'Normally I wouldn't behave like that but it was just – it wasn't planned but I just folded back on the chair and fell. I stood up and shook his hand; I didn't scatter the pieces. I usually swing on my chair because I just like it, and that was the first time I just fell down, then I stood up fast. Everything was fine, it was just the moment.' ∎

Using the New In Chess app is easy!

- get early access to every issue
- replay all games in the Gameviewer

1

Sign in with your username and password to access the digital issue.

2

Read the articles, optimized for your screen size.

3

Select a move in the text to make the chess board appear. You can analyze the games with the built-in Stockfish engine.

The only chess magazine that moves

www.newinchess.com/chess-apps – for tablet, phone and PC

Available on the App Store

Get it on Google play

What's wrong with Chess960?

In the previous issues of New In Chess, Mr van Rensburg's idea of Chess17 was widely discussed. While it is interesting and deserves practical tests, I am wondering what is wrong with Chess960?

The castling rules in Chess960 are in a way identical to standard chess, although it might take some time to get accustomed to them. Similarly, pushing 'Harry the h-pawn' (or the a-pawn), as mentioned by Mr van Rensburg, occurs in Chess960 quite frequently, particularly with queens in the corner, knights on g3 (g6, b3, b6) or with opposite-side castling.

Some Chess960 positions might appear more natural than those of Chess17, the position with queens and kings reversed being a good example.

And is it wrong when the starting position looks unusual? While I can understand that it is not pleasant to miss ♕g1xa7 on move 2 and hereby lose a piece, nor to lose material with the queen on h1 after f2-f4 f7-f5 g2-g3 and a quick ...♗g8-d5, I find it good that one needs to pay attention from the very beginning. Some experience combined with enough focus might reduce such lapses considerably.

In my opinion, Chess960 is perfectly fine in itself. It has many advantages because of the lack of theory, as the players can demonstrate their skills over the board rather than make theoretical draws after a long and tiring preparation. This is an oversimplification, but there are many good reasons why Chess960 deserves more support. Alas, it lacks sponsors and organizers.

While many leading players happily play Chess960 when there is an opportunity to participate in a prestigious event with a reasonable prize fund, such opportunities are very rare, which is a pity. Creativity, freshness, versatility and sustainability could attract sponsors. (As for sustainability, Chess960 might mean serious energy savings, as there is no need to run supercomputers for many hours during preparation.)

I am definitely not speaking about replacing standard chess, but Chess960 could well exist alongside with it.

David Navara,
Prague, Czech Republic

Pawn Breakthroughs

It is nice that GM Surya Ganguly writes about Pawn Breakthroughs (New In Chess 2021/8). It is disappointing, however, that he uses positions from others (composers) without any reference.

The first example ('Basic breakthrough') he gives is ancient – when almost nobody cared about such issues. The original (mirrored vertically, and then with w♔a2 and b♔e4) probably stems from Cozio (*Il Giuoco degli Scacchi* position 56, 1766) presented with reversed colours (Black to play and win).

The second example ('Where to hide?'), is an endgame study by my countryman Theodorus Kok (1906-1999) and was published in *De Schaakwereld* no. 44 11vii1940.

The third example ('Teamwork') was composed by the Frenchman Pierre Cathignol (1949) and won a commendation in the 1981 tourney of the French composition magazine *Thèmes-64*. It was published well before the advent of the chess computer engines and it is remarkable that it is still (seems to be) sound.

It is not difficult to find such references, as these are included in my endgame study database (www.hhdbvi. nl). Similar articles have also appeared in print elsewhere, including one by myself in the Dutch endgame study magazine *EBUR* no.2 2001). That article inspired me to try and find interesting pawn breakthroughs with fewer pawns. This is what I composed:

Harold van der Heijden
AD-Magazine 18i2003
White to play and win

1.♔h1!
The immediate breakthroughs don't work: 1.e5? fxe5 2.g5 e4 3.g6 e3 4.g7 e2 5.g8♕ e1♕ draws. After 1.g5? fxg5 White must be careful not to lose: 2.♔h3 ♔f3 and now 3.e5? g4+ 4.♔h2 ♔f2 and Black wins, but 3.♔h2 with a draw. 1.♔h3? ♔f3 forcing 2.e5 fxe5 3.g5 e4 4.g6 e3 5.g7 e2 6.g8♕ e1♕, again with a draw.
And now the black king must not block his pawn: 1...♔e3 2.e5! fxe5 3.g5 e3 4.g6, or allow a pawn to promote with check: 1...♔g3 2.e5 fxe5 3.g5. But:
1...♔f3 looks fine. However: **2.e5! fxe5 3.g5 e4** But now, as the black king cannot stop the g-pawn, the white king can stop the e-pawn by **4.♔g1! e3 5.♔f1 e2+ 6.♔e1** And wins.
But, as White made a waiting move, what is wrong with **1...♔f1** Well:
2.e5 fxe5 3.g5 e4 4.g6 e3 5.g7 e2 6.g8♕ e1♕ Draw? No! **7.♕g2** Mate.

Dr. Harold van der Heijden,
Deventer, The Netherlands

Meltdown in Dubai

The €2m World Championship match at the Dubai Expo ended in a shockingly easy victory for Magnus Carlsen. While the number of games had been increased from 12 to 14 to heighten the chances of a decisive result, only 11 games were needed when challenger Ian Nepomniachtchi had a stunning meltdown. **JONATHAN TISDALL** relives the drama and draws conclusions.

This largely ringside account of Magnus Carlsen's fifth title match needs a bit of background. I had an official role at the match; one I had never anticipated executing. The match marked my 40th anniversary as a World Championship reporter, having begun covering the 1981 Karpov-Kortchnoi rematch in Merano as a freelancer for Reuters. After that, for the next dozen years or so, I covered all major events and regularly roasted FIDE.

So it was an odd feeling to be approached by David Llada, FIDE's Chief Marketing and Communications Officer, and offered the position of FIDE Press Officer in Dubai. The opportunity to work an entire match is always very tempting, and FIDE has changed enough over the years that seeing the other side of the fence also fascinated. But I wondered if

As Magnus Carlsen pops a massive balloon and black confetti comes whirling down, Ian Nepomniachtchi knows that he will have the white pieces in Game 1.

proliferation of instant online media teams provides the next best thing nowadays. This explosion of commentary and content also becomes a part of the event, and also needs following. To try and cope, I had a minimum of three streams at low-level audio in my earphones at all times, to create a kind of cocktail party of input, hoping to be able to focus on particular 'conversations' as needed.

Subtle key points

Dubai 2021 had several modifications to the match format, which created a number of subtle key points to keep in mind. The match was expanded from 12 to 14 games, which meant a change to colour alternation. In a 12-game match, the alternation reversed at the halfway point, so that one player would have White in the first and final games, and the other, two in a row in the middle. With 14 games, there would be simple alternation, but another wrinkle: in order to maintain the actual length of the match, presumably for budgetary reasons, two rest days were eliminated and the playing schedule was 3-2-3-2-2-2.

This meant two segments where the players would have uneven colours and no natural break to prepare for the third game. And it wouldn't be until after Game 8 that there would be a break after the players would have had the same number of Whites/Blacks.

Draw offers were not allowed before move 40, and there was a novelty of great interest to veteran observers. The time limit had been changed, with controls at move 40 and 60, but with 30-second increments only in force after this. This meant 'good

it wasn't a bit odd to assign this to someone living in the champion's home country?

David explained that the media team was going to be 'quite American', with Maurice Ashley the Master of Ceremonies and TV conduit via NBC Sports, Alejandro Ramirez doing the daily video wrap, while I would produce press releases and feature reports. Besides, given the strong Russian feel of the organization... So, I took the job.

I'm a firm believer in there being no substitute for seeing a World Championship live on the spot, even if the old-fashioned' time-pressure, possibly twice. No half-minute cushion per move as time ticked away, just a truly approaching zero and harrowing scrambles if time-pressure arrived.

Popular narratives

Going into the match, a handful of factors were constantly rehashed:
– Magnus Carlsen and Ian Nepomniachtchi had a rivalry forged in their pre-teens, when the Russian had edged out the Norwegian for a couple of major junior titles. They went on to become friends, with 'Nepo' even assisting Carlsen as an analyst at major events. Despite Magnus outdistancing Ian in their adult years, the latter continues to own the best record in the world against the champ, expanding his 2-0 childhood head start to 4-1 in lifetime classical game meetings. Could a finely, finally focused Nepo spell the return of the prodigal prodigy?
– Ian is a creative and aggressive player who is naturally dangerous to Magnus, and is also buoyed by knowing he can beat the titleholder. (Magnus predicted a far more conservative challenger given the seriousness of the coming occasion.)
– Ian is a moody, reckless, streaky player who often unravels in the face of disappointment or defeat. Ian needs to raise his levels of self-discipline, and physical fitness, for the match.
– Magnus hates playing title matches, and regularly questions his ability to motivate himself for them. Magnus has massive match experience, for which there is no substitute. And, as Magnus told me in a New In Chess interview before the match, that experience is not his biggest edge. In what became a banner quote for pre-match hype, Magnus said: 'My biggest advantage in the match is that I am better at chess.'

Friendly robots

In the South Hall of the Dubai Exhibition Centre, just inside the main gateways of Expo 2020 Dubai, the

ERIC ROSEN

The spectators could watch the players in 'the fish tank', an impressive enclosure of one-way glass that allowed for full concentration. The players' rest areas and the arbiters were hidden offstage on the right.

title match was a major delayed event within a massive delayed event. The Expo was a spectacular setting, a collection of colourful global and futuristic displays amid a landscape of glittering stages and pavilions. With a high-tech profile and the motto 'Connecting Minds and Creating the Future', chess was quite a natural partner, and a cooperative effort made sense, given the challenges posed by the pandemic. With national and Expo precaution measures high – you could even be stopped and chastised by friendly robots if you loosened your mask on site – the UAE felt about as safe as possible, Covid-wise.

The match took place in 'the fish tank', an impressive enclosure of one-way glass that allowed for full concentration. Viewed from the theatre seating, the players are raised and centred, behind the middle of three massive panes, with their rest areas and the arbiters hidden offstage on the right. The audience is instructed to maintain quiet, and the lights are low, but people carry their phones and follow the in-house commentary by Vishy Anand and Anna Muzychuk in their earphones. The soundproofing was good enough that occasional Expo fireworks displays just outside the building

went unnoticed, and a slightly creaky floor in the playing area met with instant repair, the surface being re-laid between Games 1 and 2.

The first skirmish

The opening press conference was one of the livelier ones I can remember, and produced a few amusing memories and quotes. The early speech of long-time match sponsor and FIDE partner Andrey Guryev, the CEO of PhosAgro, was remarkably frank, including an apology to Magnus for the heartfelt mission and desire to return the title to Russia. Some might find this controversial, but speaking to Henrik Carlsen at the drawing of colours, the champ's father found Guryev's public confession entertainingly honest: 'Of course he does, of course they do!'

The players both appeared relaxed, confident and witty in their own ways. Nepomniachtchi was of course the more scrutinized – after all, pre-debut nerves make for guaranteed copy. He unveiled what would be his mantra on this topic, which was that once the game started, everything was normal and everything else forgotten. His reply on the expected subject of prior good relations between the two was a quotable curtain-raiser: 'Once you sit at the board, you have no friends.'

The colour ceremony took place later in the evening, with Magnus eventually popping a massive balloon that released black confetti, and gave the challenger the first move in Game 1. As mentioned before, this

'Once you sit at the board, you have no friends'

could be a slightly bigger advantage than usual, as it would also mean two whites in the first 'set', and with the players fresh, more energy to exploit them. Or, more nerves to fritter them away. There's never an easy answer.

The routines

Before the start of play, the players arrive by vehicle at the back of the exhibition hall. The Expo is not near the centre of Dubai, so this journey needs to start early to ensure traffic and security are smoothly navigated. Ian Nepomniachtchi tends to arrive in something resembling a van, with at least assistant Vladimir Potkin, manager GM Sergey Janovsky, and girlfriend Snezhana Fomicheva. The challenger emerges with earbuds, and presumably music, inserted, and his group make their way past the gathered photographers.

Magnus Carlsen travels in a car, with long-time trainer Peter Heine Nielsen, and his chum and sports podcast partner Magnus Barstad. Barstad, whom Magnus calls 'part music expert, part fashion expert, hype man', is a larger-than-life character, loudly dressed, cheerful, a mood-setter, in the Carlsen tradition of insulating the champ from match pressure with a protective layer of family and friends. If possible, Magnus prefers to linger in the car, enjoying his music and the frustration of the waiting camera-folk.

The start of play follows a daily

ritual: the voice of MC Ashley booms out of the darkness, and the players are summoned onstage from their lounges. How punctually Magnus responds is the first game of the day. The first move is ceremonially executed by a wide range of visiting dignitaries, sporting figures, sponsors. Then they are off, and we wait to see and try to interpret the first hesitations and thinks, while other observers scour for reliable theoretical intel. My own ritual is to summon the Twitterverse for predictions about the opening and the game, and this turns into a daily routine for Dutch GMs Anish Giri and Erwin l'Ami, who are happy to become regular oracles, along with a wider public.

The first set

Game 1 was a satisfying start, setting a tone of combativeness, and providing a few hints to ignite conversation. Magnus is the first to pause, treats the audience to a raising of eyebrows as he briefly contemplates the appearance of Nepo's 8th move, a version of what will turn out to be the challenger's preferred battleground as White in the first phase in Dubai, the Anti-Marshall. Clearly weighing up a choice between variations, Carlsen delights the crowd by choosing to sacrifice a pawn for active play and immediate imbalance, despite playing Black. The game is complex and tense, with equilibrium finally clear after Ian returns the pawn to shake off the strategic pressure.

In Game 2, move eight was again the first pause for Magnus, and again it appeared to be a question of choice of weaponry. Once more he opted for a pawn sacrifice, this one far sharper, and it clearly came as a surprise to Ian. A generally and sometimes overly speedy player, Nepo had played at a sensible pace in Game 1, but his early halt today hinted at trouble. The notes are by Dutch GM Jorden van Foreest, who was a member of Carlsen's team.

NOTES BY
Jorden van Foreest

Magnus Carlsen
Ian Nepomniachtchi
Dubai World Championship
2021 (Game 2)
Catalan Opening, Closed Variation

1.d4 ♘f6 2.c4 e6 3.♘f3 d5 4.g3
The Catalan is a rare guest in Magnus Carlsen's repertoire, so it might have been a slight surprise to Ian Nepomniachtchi. On the other hand, when playing a match of such magnitude, one will be ready for anything and everything.
4...♗e7 5.♗g2 0-0 6.0-0 dxc4 7.♕c2 b5 Nepomniachtchi chooses a line that has recently surged in popularity and has already acquired a reputation of being extremely solid and hard to break down.
8.♘e5

A shocker! What is overwhelmingly considered to be the main line continues with 8.a4. There, Black sacrifices a pawn but in return receives lots of piece activity. White players have not been able to prove much so far.

While looking for alternatives, we came up with this interesting idea. In essence it reverses the roles, since it is now White who sacrifices a pawn for a strong centre and piece activity.
8...c6
White's idea must have caught Nepo off-guard, because from here on in, he started spending quite some time. But he reacts very well.

9.a4 ♘d5 10.♘c3 f6!

Not the most desirable move, as it weakens the pawn structure and the king, but it is necessary to force back the knight and release some of the pressure along the long diagonal.

11.♘f3 ♕d7

Another awkward-looking but very decent move. Black is just hanging on to the extra pawn, intending to slowly develop his pieces with ...♘a6 etc.

12.e4

White definitely has to take control of the centre, although he loses control of d3 by doing so. It will be a pretty square for the black knight to sit on.

12...♘b4 13.♕e2 ♘d3

The octopus knight has arrived, but for now the other black pieces are still mainly sitting on the back rank.

14.e5! A strong concept, vacating the e4-square for the white knight. Who knows... one day it might turn into an octopus itself...

14...♗b7 This is the most human move; just getting out the pieces.

14...f5! would have been another interesting possibility, simply taking control of e4. But during the game, you can't be sure of the consequences

on the long diagonal after 15.axb5!. Now recapturing would indeed be very dangerous, but the computer suggests the calm 15...♗b7!, claiming that Black is alright, although the position definitely remains very sharp.

15.exf6! Opening up the position, which is in White's favour, since he is the player with the initiative.

15...♗xf6 The only sensible recapture, since 15...gxf6 would leave the black king without shelter.

16.♘e4 ♘a6

17.♘e5? A shocking mistake, which suddenly hands over the initiative to Black and turns the game completely on its head! Instead, White had several interesting options, retaining good compensation.

17.♘xf6+ would have been the logical continuation, setting Black a tough dilemma. Should he leave his king exposed, or allow the knight onto e5 with tempo? After 17...gxf6! (17...♖xf6 18.♘e5 looks very pleasant for White) 18.♗h6 ♖f7 19.♘e1

ANALYSIS DIAGRAM

White is the one having all the fun, although Black is certainly not out of it either.

17...♗xe5

Nepo clearly seemed surprised and blitzed out his next couple of moves quickly and confidently.

18.dxe5 ♘ac5

19.♘d6!

Probably already aware of what he had done, a horrified Carlsen thought for a while before going for this, realizing correctly that he had nothing better.

19.♘xc5 ♘xc5, and things are suddenly looking grim for White indeed, since the black knight will hop back to d3 and the diagonal will swiftly be opened with ...c6-c5.

19...♘b3

20.♖b1?

This is, in fact, the move that leaves Black objectively on top. It was possible to sacrifice the exchange in another way, leaving White with sufficient compensation for a draw: 20.♗e3! ♘xa1 21.♖xa1. It may look counter-intuitive to leave the black knight alive and the e5-pawn hanging, but White is doing fine, since Black cannot comfortably capture on e5 without allowing some tactics: 21...♘xe5 22.♗c5!

MC Maurice Ashley watches on as Magnus Carlsen and Ian Nepomniachtchi (man bun still in place) shake hands at the start of Game 2, one of the highlights of the match.

ERIC ROSEN

option, not even giving White the chance to regain any material.

24.♗e4!?

Maybe not the very best move objectively, but definitely very strong from a practical point of view. This sudden and very direct idea involves the sacrifice of the bishop on h7, followed by a rook lift to h4.

24.♘xb5 is the top engine choice, but one can understand that Carlsen felt he had no time for such trifles in this position.

24...c3? Suddenly, being faced with an attack on his king, Nepo commits a serious error, giving up his advantage. Although the desire to open the b-file is understandable, giving up a full pawn was unnecessary. Instead, there were two other options, both of which would have put White in a very difficult position.

24...bxa4!? is the first choice, not fearing any ghosts! 25.♗xh7+ (the only logical option) 25...♔xh7 26.♕h5+ ♔g8 27.♖d4 ♕e7!.

ANALYSIS DIAGRAM

22...♘d3 23.♘xb7 ♕xb7 24.♗xf8 ♖xf8 25.axb5 ♕xb5 26.♕xe6+ ♔h8 27.♖xa7, with a likely draw as a result.

20...♘bxc1 21.♖bxc1 ♘xc1 22.♖xc1

The smoke has cleared, and Black is

up a full exchange and a pawn. Yet things are far from easy due to White's piece activity. If Black managed to free his entombed bishop on b7 with ...c5, he would probably be able to convert his material advantage, so Nepo tries to achieve exactly that.

22...♖ab8! A good multi-purpose move, allowing the bishop to slide back to a8 and giving the rook potential to operate along the b-file.

23.♖d1 This makes a lot of sense – simply improving the rook.

23...♗a8?!

Definitely the most logical follow-up, as ...c5 is now finally on the cards. The cold-blooded silicon machine suggests 23...bxa4 as an interesting

ANALYSIS DIAGRAM

The point. Black gives up his queen, but stops the attack: 28.♖h4 ♕xh4 29.♕xh4 ♖xb2 30.♕xc4 ♖b1+

31.♔g2 c5+ 32.♔h3 ♗d5. Thus far, the variation has been more or less forced. White has drawing chances, but he could easily lose as well.

A more common-sense solution was 24...g6!?, stopping any ♗xh7 shenanigans, and introducing the idea of sliding the queen over to g7. Here, too, Black is very much on top.

25.♕c2?! In return, however, Carlsen himself makes a mistake. Perhaps, he felt there was no difference between this and 25.bxc3.

25...g6 26.bxc3?

Continuing his plan, but this might, in fact, very well have been a losing mistake! A complete change of plan, with ♕xc3, and allowing bxa4, was already called for.

26...bxa4?

The last mistake, after which the game finally enters some kind of equilibrium.

26...♕g7! would probably have been winning, although I have to admit that it is nearly impossible for a human to judge the resulting complications correctly, so it's very understandable that Nepo did not go for this line: 27.f4 g5!.

ANALYSIS DIAGRAM

This is the idea, breaking down the white pawn formation. White can fight in numerous ways, but nothing seems to work for him. A crucial line goes as follows: 28.♕b3 gxf4 29.♕xe6+ ♔h8 30.axb5 fxg3 31.bxc6 gxh2+ 32.♔h1 ♖f4 33.♕d7 ♖xe4 34.♘xe4 ♕g6!

ANALYSIS DIAGRAM

35.♘f6 ♗xc6+ 36.♕xc6 ♖g8!!, and Black wins. A fantastic line. Bear in mind that all black moves were necessary to achieve the win.

27.♕xa4

Despite still being down an exchange, White's pieces coordinate wonderfully, giving him full compensation at last.

27...♖fd8 28.♖a1 c5

It must have been a relief for Black to finally exchange the bishop.

29.♕c4 ♗xe4 30.♘xe4 ♔h8!

Both players play extremely accurately from this point on. Here Black dodges out of any knight forks and gets ready to infiltrate with his major pieces.

31.♘d6!

Carlsen cleverly stops any of that. The black pawns are all so weak that one of them will have to be given up.

31...♖b6 32.♕xc5 ♖db8

Intending a rook trade, which generally favours the side that is up the exchange. This is easily parried, however.

33.♔g2 a6 34.♔h3!

A pretty move – the king suddenly finds a safe haven on h3. The point is that any exchanges are avoided for the moment, leaving Black in a bind.

34...♖c6

Perhaps 34...♕c6 would have been a tad more accurate, trying to activate the queen. Still, the game remains relatively balanced, although at this point, White is already on the better side of the draw.

35.♕d4 ♔g8 36.c4 ♕c7

37.♕g4

A decision that surprised many – allowing Black to simplify just before the time-control. Later Carlsen said that he did not see any way to improve his position.

37.♔g2 is the best try I could find, intending h4-h5; but then again, this is easily dealt with by 37...♖f8, intending ...♕b6.

37...♖xd6 38.exd6 ♕xd6 39.c5

This, although it wins a pawn, is in essence a draw offer, since an elementary 3 vs 2 rook ending cannot be avoided. Perhaps, 39.♔g2 could have been tried, once again intending h4-h5, but it would not have been much, that's for sure.

39...♕xc5 40.♕xe6+ ♔g7 41.♖xa6

41...♖f8!

A final accurate move. A queen trade cannot really be avoided, and the game ended not long afterwards.

42.f4 ♕f5+ 43.♕xf5 ♖xf5 44.♖a7+ ♔g8 45.♔g4 ♖b5 46.♖e7 ♖a5 47.♖e5 ♖a7 48.h4 ♔g7 49.h5 ♔h6 50.♔h4 ♖a1 51.g4 ♖h1+ 52.♔g3 gxh5 53.♖e6+ ♔g7 54.g5 ♖g1+ 55.♔f2 ♖a1 56.♖h6 ♖a4

57.♔f3 ♖a3+ 58.♔f2 ♖a4

An intense struggle, and certainly one of the most interesting games of the match, with many ups and downs!

■ ■ ■

There is of course a huge temptation to see trends in two games, no matter how foolish that might be. To sum up the easily jumped-to conclusions, we can decide that Magnus has so far been better prepared, more aggressively (or ambitiously) prepared, and is clearly pursuing the 'swing hard early' strategy.

More confusing was the apparent lack of depth of preparation behind Carlsen's wicked opening surprise, which could mean: Magnus was armed with many ways to surprise but these did not produce definite paths to advantage; or that Nepo had improvised his way to playable confusion.

Nepo must surely gain bonus points for creating serious winning chances as Black, especially under the circumstances, while Magnus's recovery from a serious oversight shows his nerve and focus are in

Celeb 64

John Henderson

Tim Krabbé

Of all the celebs to appear here, Dutch journalist and novelist Tim Krabbé is the one with the highest degree of chess talent. Before he became famous for his written work, he was already known in chess circles as a competitive player who harboured designs on the Grandmaster title in his youth.

But Tim exchanged his chess pieces for a bicycle to become a competitive cyclist, and met with wide acclaim when he penned the cult cycling classic *The Rider* (1978). His big breakthrough followed with his psychological thriller *Het Gouden Ei* (1984), which was published in English as *The Vanishing*, and adapted into film in both The Netherlands and then Hollywood (with Jeff Bridges and Keifer Sutherland). A further novella, *The Cave* (2000), was also turned into a film.

As a chess player, Krabbé competed in two Dutch Championships, in 1967 and 1971. But he is best known to chess lovers for his writings for *Schaakbulletin* and New In Chess, and his book *Chess Curiosities* (1985), based on two similarly entitled Dutch books about what he calls 'the odder side of chess'. An early adapter to online chess publishing, he has his fascinating self-named website *Tim Krabbé's Chess Curiosities*, a veritable treasure trove of chess news, shared stories, records, personalities and problems/studies, including his chronicled research into 'the Holy Grail of Chess', Leonid Yarosh's Babson Task. ■

place – if not full accuracy. The game was a thrilling fight, with both players at their best under pressure and a bit shakier when taking the reins. The only thing I felt sure of at this point was that this was indeed shaping up to be a great match...

The fact that this game didn't produce a victor gave rise to a contentious tweet about the five-year gap since the last decisive game in a title match, which puts the most negative spin possible regarding an event that takes place every other year and has now been postponed one extra due to Covid. It is, of course, an inevitably recurring topic regarding classical World Championships, but you can hardly get a better advertisement for the enjoyment potential of a split decision than Game 2.

Having said that, the day after a nerve-wracking slugfest is odds-on to be a dud. Opening probing resumed with Nepo trying a different Anti-Marshall, Magnus ruffling through his mental database on move eight, and picking his variation of the day. The adventure levels were indeed turned down, with Carlsen now choosing a shield rather than a weapon, adopting the traditional black approach of methodical neutralization, which he achieved with care and precision.

The press conference after Game 3 produced a Carlsen classic. FIDE's social media followers produced the session's final question of the day, directed at the champion, wondering how he thought he would be remembered in 50 years' time. Carlsen said he didn't think his legacy was something to discuss during a World Championship match, before riffing on the topic of the lack of decisive results in recent title matches: 'Hopefully, as someone who won a classical game in a World Championship match after 2016!'

The first rest day arrived, but the colours did not yet balance, the next set being two games long.

Mission accomplished. The old and new champion together with his chum Magnus Barstad ('part music expert, part fashion expert, hype man') after the prize-giving.

A new commentator fixation

The challenger's dilemma – dress up for the occasion and iron out one's flaws, or let one's hair down and ride on one's strengths? While commentating today for Chess24, Anish Giri voiced something that certainly struck a nerve with the average chess fan, and which would quickly become a major obsession when Nepomniachtchi's match repertoire became clearer: 'He has been playing this as a neutral top player so far... It would be more fun to see quick Ian, impulsive Ian, attacking Ian... For now we see a very well-prepared player who doesn't take any risks, doesn't put any pressure on the clock, double/triple checks his moves.'

I can hear some traditional Soviet authority figure digging Anish out for requesting 'fun' during a title match. And as Ian gradually became faster and more impulsive in Dubai, things would go wrong. But there is more than a purely spectator's desire to see action and risk from someone else's precious title challenge: Ian is viewed as, and associated with, 'fun' chess. The key ingredient in that quote for me is 'attacking'. What seems to be missing from title Ian is aggression.

Nothing sums up spectator frustration, and the spectre of endless draws, like the Petroff Defence, and no opening seems more foreign to Nepo's nature. But in a match setting, its sterility is a different kind of weapon. We know it proved an impenetrable wall and a near match-winner for Fabiano Caruana in the all-draw title duel of 2018 in London, and a few intervening years of supercomputer number-crunching would only have made it even more effective. In the press conference after Game 4, Magnus would say the Petroff was no surprise, since Ian had used it to consolidate his victory at the Candidates, even winning with it vs. Wang Hao.

Nepo's smooth and obviously nearly completely prepared neutralization of 1.e4 cemented a growing narrative. The presence of Sergey Karjakin as a team second revived memories of the long series of draws in New York 2016 that eventually provoked a frustrated implosion from Carlsen and the near-loss of his title.

The seductive argument is that this strategy is in play here, with Karjakin convincing his compatriot that not losing is the key to winning the match, and a growing suspicion that this will fit Nepomniachtchi like an itchy suit. For now, though, Team Nepo is looking well prepared, and have already achieved one major counterpunching opportunity (in Game 2).

More than meets the eye

Watching Game 5 from a distance, or replaying it in retrospect, would most likely give an impression of match deadlock, another typical high-level tussle characterized by subtle defensive ideas. Looking deeper, and off the board and into their heads, there is an argument for this being a pivotal moment, and a stage-setter for what would prove to be the final showdown.

For the first time, Nepo prep produced a tangible advantage, and Magnus appeared visibly uncomfortable. The key moment is hard to notice viewed from afar, but Ian's decision on move 20 seemed terribly eloquent. This marked his first long think, and instead of playing the most obvious and promising move, he produced a minimalist choice that allowed Carlsen to start whittling his way to equality. Ian was terse and irritable as the scoresheets were signed, and gave the impression that this felt more annoying than the missed opportunities in Game 2.

Ian Nepomniachtchi
Magnus Carlsen
Dubai World Championship
2021 (Game 5)

position after 19...♕e8

Here Nepomniachtchi went:
20.♖ed1?!
20.c4 was widely anticipated by commentators and observers, and indeed it generates a very unpleasant initiative. Afterwards even Ian seemed a bit puzzled about how he avoided such a natural and straight-forward move. It was also easy for pundits to interpret this as a side-effect of the presumed match strategy of provocation through extreme conservatism.
20...♗e6 21.♗a4 ♗d7 22.♘d2 ♗xa4 23.♕xa4 ♕xa4 24.♖xa4 ♖a8 25.♖da1 ♖xa4 26.♖xa4 ♖b8

And the game ended in a draw after move 43.

Pundits interpreted Nepomniachtchi's indecisive 20th move as the strait-jacket of his ill-fitting match strategy, reining in his natural instincts and literally slowing him down.

In a pre-match podcast interview with Magnus Barstad, Carlsen had been both open and detailed about how he saw his opponent, and even admitted to advising Ian in years gone by to work on his discipline: '... to handle the setbacks that will come, regardless of whether it's a good position he fails to convert, or a game that he should have held to a draw but ends up losing, or opening preparation that goes wrong – that will be a huge challenge for him.'

For now, time for another rest day, and a chance to recharge for greater efforts...

Game 6 delivers again

Statistically speaking, Game 6 of a title match tends to be both eventful and decisive, and in Dubai it also proved historic. The longest-ever title match game, it literally produced roughly three games worth of content and several dramatic scenarios, and effectively decided the contest.

NOTES BY
Jan Timman

Magnus Carlsen
Ian Nepomniachtchi
Dubai World Championship
2021 (Game 6)
Queen's Pawn Opening, Pseudo-Catalan

After the first five games in Dubai had ended in as many draws, some people were grumbling, inevitably followed by suggestions that classical chess is dead. There was no reason to panic, however. In the first Petrosian-Spassky match of 1966, the first six games were drawn, which just showed how evenly matched the combatants were.

You could say that the first five games slightly favoured the challenger on aggregate. In my preview, I had pointed out that Nepomniachtchi's chances lay in clever preparation. It was understandable, therefore, that in Game 6, Carlsen was anxious to get out of established theory as quickly as possible. That worked – but it failed to yield him an advantage!

1.d4 ♘f6 2.♘f3 d5 3.g3 e6 4.♗g2 ♗e7 5.0-0 0-0 6.b3

The first interesting moment. Carlsen goes for an uncommon move, apparently intending to lead the game into unknown territory.

6...c5 The most natural reaction.
7.dxc5 ♗xc5

8.c4 A new move. Thus far, White had always played the obvious 8.♗b2, after which White's chances of an opening advantage are negligible.
8...dxc4

Black could also have continued his development with 8...♘c6, after which the game transposes to the Tarrasch Defence.

9.♕c2 ♕e7 10.♘bd2

An interesting pawn sacrifice, and also the only way to play for an advantage. After 10.♕xc4 b6 Black would have no problems.

10...♘c6

Black could have gone for 10...cxb3. After 11.♘xb3 ♗d6 12.♘fd4 ♖d8 13.♗b2 White has sufficient compensation, but no more.

11.♘xc4

11...b5

A sharp reaction. He could also have played in the centre with 11...e5. This is slightly more committal than the

text, but there's nothing wrong with it. A possible continuation is: 12.♗b2 e4 13.♘g5 ♗f5 14.♘e3 ♗xe3 15.fxe3 ♗g6 16.♗xf6 gxf6 17.♘xe4 ♖fe8 18.♖f4 f5, and Black regains the pawn with a reasonable position.

12.♘ce5

Virtually forced, although the fact that Carlsen thought about it for 20 minutes suggests that his preparation had been somewhat short of perfect.

12...♘b4!

The point of the previous move, based on the old rule that two knights covering each other – the white ones in this case – are not very well positioned.

13.♕b2 ♗b7

14.a3

Sharper was 14.♗g5, intending to meet 14...h6 with 15.♗h4. The critical move then is 15...g5, of course, after which White has the following possibilities:

– 16.a3! gxh4 (not 16...♘bd5 in view of 17.♘xg5 hxg5 18.♗xg5, and the pin is lethal) 17.axb4 ♗xb4 18.♘d3 ♘d5, and the position is equal.

– 16.♘xg5 ♗xg2 17.♘h7 (not 17.♔xg2 in view of 17...hxg5 18.♗xg5 ♕b7+)

17...♔xh7 18.♘g4 ♘bd5 19.♕d2 ♗e3 20.fxe3 ♘e4 21.♕xd5 exd5 22.♗xe7 ♗xf1 23.♖xf1 ♖g8, and Black has a slight plus.

14...♘c6 15.♘d3 ♗b6 16.♗g5 ♖fd8 17.♗xf6

A justified swap. White gives up the bishop pair in order to slightly weaken Black's pawn structure. After 17.♖ac1 ♘d4 18.♗xf6 Black could recapture with the queen, although this wouldn't upset the balance either: after 18...♕xf6 19.♘xd4 ♗xd4 20.♕d2 the bishop swap is inevitable, after which the knight is no worse than the bishop.

17...gxf6

During the game, some commentators suggested that Nepomniachtchi was playing to win here, and it's true that Black has absolutely nothing to fear after 17...♕xf6 18.♕xf6 gxf6 19.♖fc1 ♖ac8. By recapturing with the pawn, Black is hoping to demonstrate that the white queen is not well-placed on b2. But in both cases, with or without the queens, the position is equal.

18.♖ac1 ♘d4

The alternative was 18...e5 19.♘h4 ♘d4, winning space in the centre. White's best bet now is probably 20.b4, aiming for control of square c5.

19.♘xd4 ♗xd4 20.♕a2 ♗xg2 21.♔xg2 ♕b7+ 22.♔g1 ♕e4 23.♕c2 a5 24.♖fd1 ♔g7 25.♖d2

Carlsen keeps manoeuvring without exposing himself in the least. The alternative was 25.e3. After 25...♗e5 26.♕e2 h5 27.h4 ♕g4 the position is equal.

Ian Nepomniachtchi realizes it's going to be a long and tough night. Lasting 136 moves, Game 6 was the longest title match game ever.

25...♖ac8 A tempting move, but one I'd never have played myself. With open files, two rooks tend to be stronger than the queen. Here it's actually not too bad, since Black's queen and bishop are very actively placed, and are helping to maintain the balance. There is a potential danger, however, which will show itself later in the game: the rooks might break loose and penetrate via the open files with hardly any danger for White, mainly because of Black's weakened kingside structure.

Instead of the text, 25...b4 would have been an excellent move. Black is threatening to play his bishop to c3, forcing White to capture twice on b4.

After 26.axb4 axb4 27.♘xb4 ♗xf2+ 28.♔xf2 ♕xb4 the position is equal.

26.♕xc8 ♖xc8 27.♖xc8 ♕d5 28.b4 a4 Fixing the white a-pawn. 28...e5 was also possible, after which Black threatens to further advance his e-pawn, giving White no time to capture on a5. A possible continuation is 29.e3 ♗xe3 30.fxe3 axb4 31.axb4 e4 32.♖c5 ♕d7 33.♖c3 ♕d6, and a draw is looming.

29.e3 Remarkably enough, Carlsen now plays this committal pawn move anyway. With 29.♖cc2 he could have forced Black to play extremely accurately: only 29...♕b3! 30.♘c1 ♕b1 would have preserved the balance.

Prof Stuart Russell: 'We're setting up a chess match between ourselves and the machines – with the fate of the world as a prize.' *(The eminent British AI expert in his 2021 Reith Lectures, 'Living with Artificial Intelligence')*

IM Levy Rozman: 'The biggest circus in chess is around 1200. Some days, you play like a 400 and all your pieces disappear. Other days you are 1800 level, converting games flawlessly.' *(Tweeted by the prolific Twitch and YouTube broadcaster, aka Gotham Chess)*

David Bronstein: 'The most powerful weapon in chess is to have the next move.'

Jonathan Penrose: '[...] like playing an Essex versus Middlesex county match.' *(Typically downplaying his famous victory over reigning World Champion Mikhail Tal at the Leipzig Olympiad in 1960. Sadly, the 10-time British champion died in late November, aged 88)*

Jamie Njoku-Goodwin: 'Chess is a universal religion. Its devotees are weird and wonderful people. Sometimes eccentric, often obsessive, always interesting, they also tend to know far more about their cities than most.' *(From the chief executive of UK Music, and a former special government adviser at the Department for Health and Social Care, in his*

feature The weird and wonderful world of underground chess, in the November 13 issue for The Spectator magazine)

Eva Babitz: 'I had thrown my body in for art. I had thrown myself into this game for art. You know, I was not a very good artist. But this was, like, one thing I could do.' *(The cult writer/muse died in December aged 78. As a young free-wheeling student, she became famous for being photographed playing a chess match nude against Dada pioneer Marcel Duchamp in 1963, during his retrospective at the Pasadena Museum of Art)*

Mikhail Tal: 'But Botvinnik is a chess artist, and I am an adventurer.' *(In an interview during the 1990 Novi Sad Olympiad)*

Siegbert Tarrasch: 'What is the object of playing a gambit opening? ... To acquire a reputation of being a dashing player at the cost of losing a game.'

Peter Hitchens: 'Will there be war in Ukraine? It is an incredibly valuable piece of territory, a vital square on the Giant Chessboard of Europe. Whoever controls it gains huge political, military and economic benefits.' *(The polemic author and reporter in his December 18 column for the Mail on Sunday)*

Vishy Anand: 'There are some things we do much better than

computers, but since most of chess is tactically based they do many things better than humans. And this imbalance remains. I no longer have any issues. It's a bit like asking an astronomer, does he mind that a telescope does all the work. He is used to it. It is just an incredible tool that you can use.'

Professor Robert Desjarlais: 'Chess gets a hold of some people, like a virus or a drug.' *(In the chess-loving academic's 2012 book, Counterplay: An Anthropologist at the Chessboard)*

Evgeny Bareev: 'I think maybe I didn't get enough different skills. That makes me very sad.' *(The Soviet-born Grandmaster and now Canada's top player, philosophically reflecting on his chess career and life choices, interviewed for The Globe And Mail in mid-December)*

G.H. Hardy: 'Chess problems are the hymn-tunes of mathematics.' *(The popular early 20th-century English mathematician, famed for his achievements in number theory and mathematical analysis)*

Ze'ev Elkin MP: 'I've fulfilled a childhood dream and played against my hero and a chess world champion, from whom I've learned to love the game.' *(The Israeli Housing and Construction Minister, after playing against Garry Kasparov in late November during an international innovativeness conference in Jerusalem)*

29...♗e5 30.h4 h5 31.♔h2 ♗b2
At this point, Carlsen had only three minutes left for nine moves, which probably explains the text – played to cause confusion. Objectively, this move is a serious error.
With 31...♕b3 Black could have preserved the balance. A possible continuation is: 32.♖xe5 fxe5 33.♖d7 ♕xa3 34.♖cc7 ♕b2 35.♖xf7+ ♔g6, and White has no more than perpetual check.
32.♖c5 Played immediately.
32...♕d6

33.♖d1
With so little time left, it was hard to see that White could have got a winning advantage with 33.♖cc2! ♗xa3 34.♘f4!. The main variation goes as follows: 34...♕xb4 35.♖d7 e5 36.♘xh5+ ♔g6, and now the piece sac 37.♖c6! wins. Giri pointed out that this last move was very hard to see. With enough time, Carlsen would probably have found it.
33...♗xa3 34.♖xb5 ♕d7 35.♖c5

35...e5 Nepomniachtchi seems to be continuing to play slightly out-of-the-way moves to exploit White's time-trouble. Just taking the b-pawn

would have made more sense: after 35...♗xb4 36.♖cc1 ♗a5 37.♘e5 ♕b5 38.♘c6 ♗b6 39.♘d4 ♕a5 Black keeps his passed pawn. But White will have little trouble defending his position.
36.♖c2 With 36.e4, White could have prevented the capture on b4, but I think Carlsen had decided to keep his structure intact – even at the cost of a pawn.
36...♕d5 A strange move. There really wasn't the slightest reason now not to play 36...♗xb4, since Black could have met 37.♖cc1 ♗a3 38.♖a1 with the power move 38...♕g4!, and although Black now keeps his a-pawn, White needn't despair. There could follow: 39.♖d2 ♗f8 40.♖da2 a3 41.♘e1 ♗e7 42.♘c2 f5 43.♘xa3 f4 44.♘c2, and White holds.
37.♖dd2 ♕b3 38.♖a2 The position is now dynamically balanced.

38...e4 A serious mistake. Black should have gone 38...f5. If White then continues with 39.♘c5 ♕xb4 40.♖dc2, Black breaks open the kingside with 40...f4, guaranteeing a draw.
39.♘c5 ♕xb4

40.♘xe4 The last move in time-trouble. Carlsen settles for a pawn,

which is a good practical choice. If he had had more time, however, he wouldn't have missed that 40.♖dc2! would have forced a technically winning position. This rook move is extra strong now in view of Black's inability to create counterplay on the kingside. In fact, Black is powerless in the face of the threat 41.♘xa4 ♕xa4 42.♖c3. White wins the bishop, and Black is doomed, even with only pawns on the kingside. White can calmly double rooks on the seventh rank and take on f7. To prevent this, Black must launch a desperate attack, e.g. 40...f5 41.♘xa4 f4 (41...♕xa4 42.♖c3) 42.exf4 e3 43.fxe3 ♕b3 44.♘c3 ♗c5 45.♖ab2 ♕a3 46.e4 ♕a1, and now the simple 47.♘b1 is enough. White wins.
40...♕b3
Nepomniachtchi understandably wants to correct his mistake on move 39, but there was no reason here to play the queen. The computer regards the position after 40...♔g6! as fully equal.
41.♖ac2 ♗f8 And here 41...f5 suggested itself. After 42.♘c5 ♕b5 43.♘d3 ♕b3, again neither player can play for a win.
42.♘c5 ♕b5 43.♘d3 a3 44.♘f4 ♕a5 45.♖a2 ♗b4 46.♖d3 ♔h6
Covering the h-pawn and giving his queen the freedom of the board again.
47.♖d1 ♕a4 48.♖da1
Doubling the rooks does not cause any immediate threats, but Carlsen is still waiting for a slight inaccuracy on Black's part.
48...♗d6 49.♔g1 ♕b3 50.♘e2 ♕d3 51.♘d4 ♔h7 52.♔h2

52...♕e4 A careless move offering White new starting-points. With, for example, 52...♔h6, Black could easily have held this position.

53.♖xa3! Of course. White is quite happy to invest an exchange in eliminating the annoying a-pawn.

53...♕xh4+ Black's best chance. If he had captured on a3, his weak structure would end up costing him the game.

54.♔g1 ♕e4 55.♖a4

A new phase has started. With the enemy pawn gone, White can play for a win without risking anything.

55...♗e5 56.♘e2 ♕c2 57.♖1a2 ♕b3 58.♔g2 ♕d5+

59.f3

This pawn move took the commentators by surprise. They had expected White to preserve his structure with 59.♔h2. The text has both pros and cons: on the one hand, White gains some space; on the other, he has created a target (pawn e3) for the black bishop.

59...♕d1 60.f4 ♗c7

Black is going to take his bishop to b6 in order to target the white e-pawn. The alternative was 60...♗b2 61.♔f2

♕b1, and White will find it hard to make progress.

61.♔f2 ♗b6 62.♖a1 ♕b3 63.♖e4 ♔g7 64.♖e8 f5 65.♖aa8 ♕b4 66.♖ac8 ♗a5 67.♖c1 ♗b6 68.♖e5 ♕b3 69.♖e8 ♕d5 70.♖cc8 ♕h1

'Draw incoming', Ganguly observed at this point. But we're not there yet by a long stretch.

71.♖c1 ♕d5 72.♖b1

White continues his patient manoeuvring, hoping for a careless moment from Black.

72...♗a7

With 72...♗c7, Black could have prevented the following transaction.

73.♖e7 ♗c5 74.♖e5 ♕d3 75.♖b7 ♕c2 76.♖b5 ♗a7 77.♖a5 ♗b6 78.♖ab5 ♗a7

79.♖xf5 Carlsen sees a new chance. He is aiming for a technical endgame that will be very difficult for Black to defend over the board.

79...♕d3 80.♖xf7+!

The point of the previous move.

80...♔xf7 81.♖b7+ ♔g6 82.♖xa7

The start of the final phase. White will have to try to set his connected passed pawns in motion, which will

inevitably give Black new queen checks. The swap of the white g-pawn for the black h-pawn will also be unavoidable. This leaves the position still objectively drawn, but the defence will be 'hell' for Black, as Judit Polgar said in her live commentary.

82...♕d5 83.♖a6+ ♔h7 84.♖a1 ♔g6 85.♘d4 ♕b7 86.♖a2 ♕h1 87.♖a6+ ♔f7 88.♘f3 ♕b1 89.♖d6 ♔g7 90.♖d5 ♕a2+ 91.♖d2 ♕b1 92.♖e2 ♕b6 93.♖c2 ♕b1 94.♘d4 ♕h1 95.♖c7+ ♔f6 96.♖c6+ ♔f7 97.♘f3 ♕b1 98.♘g5+ ♔g7 99.♘e6+ ♔f7 100.♘d4 ♕h1 101.♖c7+ ♔f6 102.♘f3

After a long journey the knight is back where it started. White is going to try a new tack.

102...♕b1 103.♖d7 ♕b2+ 104.♖d2 ♕b1 105.♘g1 ♕b4 106.♖d1 ♕b3 107.♖d6+ ♔g7 108.♖d4 ♕b2+ 109.♘e2 ♕b1 110.e4

White finally gets his pawns moving – but only one step for now.

110...♕h1 111.♖d7+ ♔g8 112.♖d4 ♕h2+ 113.♔e3 h4

Forcing a pawn swap. The endgame that now arises can be checked against the tablebase at any point. For the moment, it's still a draw.

114.gxh4 ♕h3+ 115.♔d2 ♕xh4 116.♖d3 ♔f8 117.♖f3 ♕d8+ 118.♔e3 ♕a5 The most accurate move was 118...♕b6+. As Carlsen explained afterwards, it would have been wiser to prevent White from transferring his knight to g3. The black queen check would have upset White's piece coordination.

119.♔f2 ♕a7+ 120.♖e3 ♕d7 121.♘g3

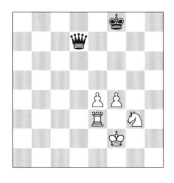

Square g3 is the ideal position for the knight at this point. All kinds of queen checks have been rendered impossible, allowing White to reinforce his position at his leisure.

121...♕d2+ 122.♔f3 ♕d1+ 123.♖e2 ♕b3+ 124.♔g2

The checks have been exhausted, which makes Blacks defensive job all the harder.

124...♕b7 125.♖d2 ♕b3 126.♖d5 ♔e7 127.♖e5+ ♔f7 128.♖f5+ ♔e8 129.e5 Another little step. **129...♕a2+ 130.♔h3**

130...♕e6

It's past midnight, and already the day of Game 7, when Magnus Carlsen tries to sum up what happened in the epic Game 6.

And finally Nepomniachtchi slips up. The only two moves were 130...♕b1 and 130...♕c2. The queen has to stay at a distance, and it's also important to keep targeting the rook. This means that 130...♕d2 would lose to 131.♘h5!, allowing White to continue to reinforce his position.

131.♘h4 131.♔g4 would have won as well. **131...♕h6+ 132.♘h5** Now the game is playing itself. **132...♕h7 133.e6**

The death blow.

133...♕g6 134.♖f7 ♔d8 135.f5 ♕g1 136.♘g7

Black resigned.

■ ■ ■

As Henrik Carlsen put it: 'I don't think I have seen Magnus as elated after a chess game in many, many years.'

My immediate reaction to this exhausting feast of a game was that it was very much a mutual effort, with both players clearly trying to inject life and tension into a position that could easily have fizzled out. Nepo's decisions to avoid an exchange of queens and then to offer a material imbalance made his ambition clear, and if anything, it was his urge to play quickly that truly let him down. In short, he was ready to be more 'himself' than people were crediting.

It is worth noting that, live on the spot, Dubai very much felt like a historic match with great potential, with small margins being the difference. It will be fascinating to see when and by how much Nepo will turn up the volume, now that he must, was my feeling at this stage.

In fact, what would be decisive was the explanation for what produced the small margins – Magnus' relentless focus and nerve.

'Rest day'

Game 7 was predictable, especially considering that the exertions of Game 6 actually lasted into the beginning of this day. Exhausted and cautious, the players circled to an uneventful draw, a positive result for Carlsen, who could progress to another White and close out the 'third set' from a position of strength.

The statistics to stew over now, particularly if you are a trailing challenger, are Carlsen's invincibility numbers. Besides holding the longest-ever undefeated streak at the elite level (125 games) he had only lost two games in his 4.5 title matches so far. The halfway mark of Dubai 2021 also meant that Carlsen would have more Whites the rest of the way, and having opened up a lead, he no longer had to take any risks – only exploit nerves and errors.

The beginning of the end

From this point, and writing after the fact, the match no longer needs to be covered in strict day-by-day fashion. Games 8-11 feel more like a cataclysmic crescendo, and analysing the self-destruction of the challenger the only subject worth discussing. The collapse began small, with both players still looking a bit worn out.

The opening of Game 8 was full of mind games; Magnus returned to 1.e4, presumably to either learn what Team Nepo had brought as their fighting defence, or to demonstrate the implausibility of the challenger ever generating a chance as Black in a Petroff. When Ian stuck to his guns, he signalled continuing patience with his match situation, but soon decided to make the murkiest out of an optically dull variation. Carlsen got more

than expected, and Nepo appeared slightly disjointed, torn between wanting to get out safely and making something happen. Which might explain this:

Magnus Carlsen
Ian Nepomniachtchi
Dubai World Championship
2021 (Game 8)

position after 21.♗xc4

The stage is set for blunder number one. White's temporary initiative is under control after something like 21...♔g8 but after:
21...b5?? Black just loses a pawn, without compensation.
22.♕a3+ ♔g8 As 22...♕d6 23.♕xa7 bxc4 runs into 24.♕a8+.
23.♕xa7

And Carlsen converted smoothly after:

23...♕d8 24.♗b3 ♖d6 25.♖e4 ♗e6 26.♗xe6 ♖xe6 27.♖xe6 fxe6 28.♕c5 ♕a5 29.♕xc6 ♕e1+ 30.♔h2 ♕xf2 31.♕xe6+ ♔h7 32.♕e4+ (1-0, 46)

After the blunder, Ian spent more and more of his time offstage, and as Magnus tightened the technical clamp, the challenger spent some of his rare time at the board with his head rested on the table, a picture of defeat. Carlsen admitted afterwards that he had been completely puzzled by his adversary's decisions, and had planned to just do some gentle testing and probing, with an eye on keeping a draw in hand and reaching the rest day.

The more things change...

While the task facing Nepomniachtchi now felt statistically hopeless (with the score 5-3), there was still a sense of change and excitement when the battle recommenced, with the players recharged. Sergey Karjakin had reappeared, flown back in to provide some sort of advisory and morale boost, and Ian had shed his topknot, disgraced samurai style. Magnus appeared to be mysteriously jumpy during the early stage of the game, and there was a widespread sense of anticipation that at least NOW, we would finally see a released and swashbuckling Nepo.

The first phase of the game fanned the mood, with Nepo choosing relatively non-theoretical waters after switching to 1.c4, Magnus cooperating with a fairly unusual system, then thorough Russian prep gradually emerging as the challenger played quickly and actively, clearly ready even for this backwater. Karjakin was enthusiastic about the on-the board state of affairs, predicting real action, when Ian suddenly surprised him, and many commentators, with another relatively tame decision on move 15.

Carlsen 'accidentally' gave up a pawn later in the game, but the strategic soundness of his overall plan gifted him full compensation. Then this happened:

As Magnus tightened the technical clamp, the challenger spent some of his rare time at the board with his head rested on the table, a picture of defeat

Ian Nepomniachtchi, Magnus Carlsen

Dubai World Championship 2021 (Game 9)

position after 26...♖a4

Black's active pieces and the targets on a2, c4 and e5 give him full compensation for the lost pawn. There is one other target in the position...

27.c5?? c6!

White's ♗b7 is not getting out alive, and White's last move ensured this by taking away the c5-square from his knight. Carlsen finished with surgical precision.

28.f3 ♘h6 29.♖e4 ♖a7 30.♖b4 ♖b8 31.a4 ♖axb7

32.♖b6 ♖xb6 33.cxb6 ♖xb6 34.♘c5 ♘f5 35.a5 ♖b8 36.a6 ♘xg3 37.♘a4 c5 38.a7 ♖d8 39.♘xc5 ♖a8 0-1.

The champ's eyes nearly popped out of his head when he saw White's 27th, and after some very visibly perplexed faces, Magnus added a black win to his collection, opened up a three-point lead, and finally erased his career deficit against Nepo. The score was now 5-4 in his favour.

The game also contained a mini-furore, the traditional match 'j'adoubegate', where the cameras spot a player gripping a piece before moving another. This year's edition had a bit more spice to it, since Nepo was offstage when it happened, Magnus apparently not announcing the adjustment since he was alone at the board, the arbiters noting it as a clear adjustment ... and a recent rule change.

FIDE has changed the wording of the touch-move rule to allow for absurdly strict interpretation, potentially even accidental brushing of a piece counting as touched. Elite players, events and arbiters continue to know the difference between adjusting and planning to move, but the rule needs to be reset. A protest was actually filed eventually, but too late and incorrectly, and was dismissed.

Games 10-11. No fun at all

Even Magnus was startled by the appearance of yet another Petroff in Game 10, but as one of the match's duller draws unfolded, perhaps a day of safety followed by one of rest was just what the challenger needed. The match is beyond reach, and it is only a question of what kind of consolation Ian seeks.

And then came Game 11.

BEFORE AND DURING GAME 9...

NOTES BY
Peter Heine Nielsen

Ian Nepomniachtchi
Magnus Carlsen
Dubai World Championship
2021 (Game 11)
Italian Game, Giuoco Pianissimo

Chess is a strange sport, in the sense that a World Championship can be practically decided, yet will go on for days. In football, if you lead 3-0 in the World Cup final, it will be a matter of minutes and in basketball or baseball you might be down 3-0 in games needing to win 4 in a row, but with there being no draws, it mathematically still comes down to a 6% chance. In chess it is quite different. Mathematical models gave Magnus more than 99.9% to retain his title when he was leading 6½-3½ with four games to go. There even was a free day before Game 11 to drag things out even further. We tried to stick to our routines, preparing for the game exactly as usual, and I,

1.e4 e5!
A trend in recent World Championship history has been the ability just to repeat one's openings as Black, without getting hit by preparation of the opposing team. To Garry Kasparov the quote has been attributed that any solid opening only holds up for three games in a match, and while that might have been true in his time, with modern computers it seems that Black basically can just stay and trust his preparation, putting the burden fully on White to show any kind of idea to get the game going. Fabiano Caruana and Ian Nepomniachtchi successfully repeated the Petroff for a full match, Magnus the Marshall in both 2016 and 2021. The Sveshnikov, of course, had its bad moment in 2018, but also created numerous winning chances and was therefore a much more combative choice, balancing risk and reward. Modern engines play a huge part, making analysis more exact and making it possible to almost mathematically map out areas, especially

The slow nature of the Italian Game allows Black some flexibility with move orders, as White has no immediate threats. Magnus's choice is rather rare, and at first sight it might indeed seem odd to play ...♗a7 and ...a5 before castling or ...h6. Still, it forces White to show his hand, besides obviously trying to get him out of his specific preparation.
8.♘a3 h6 9.♘c2
9.♘b5 is logical, but after 9...♗b6 ...♘e7 and ...c6 come next, forcing White to take immediate action, if he doesn't want to be pushed back.
9...0-0 10.♗e3 ♗xe3 11.♘xe3 ♖e8 12.a4 ♗e6 13.♗xe6 ♖xe6

The idea that Magnus should suddenly lose three of the next four games felt very remote when they sat down for Game 11

if anyone, vividly remembered the 2008 match in which Vishy Anand held a comfortable 3-point lead over Vladimir Kramnik with three games to go, and recalled the mood change when it suddenly became +2, with only one game as White left.
Still, these days, wins in a World Championship are a rarity, and Magnus's last loss in a title match dated back to more than 5(!) years ago, and the total number of his losses was two in five matches.
Therefore, the idea that he should suddenly lose three of the next four games indeed felt very remote when the players sat down for Game 11 with the score at 6½-3½.

as nowadays even neural networks are added to the equation. Traditionally, as a match progressed, a black repertoire became more and more exposed, but these days it seems to matter less, as White seems unable to exploit it.
2.♘f3 ♘c6 3.♗c4!?
Earlier in the match the challenger stuck to the Ruy Lopez, and while getting nominal advantages, they were of the kind that evaporated with exact play from Black. The Italian Game has seen a renaissance in recent years, leading to playable positions of a less forcing nature.
3...♘f6 4.d3 ♗c5 5.c3 d6 6.0-0 a5 7.♖e1 ♗a7!?

One can make the argument that White is slightly better. His structure is moderately preferable, the knight at e3 a bit better placed than the one at c6. Still, as in the comment above, such advantages are of a temporary nature if Black plays well.
14.♕b3 b6 15.♖ad1 ♘e7 16.h3 ♕d7 17.♘h2 ♖d8!
Magnus thought quite a while before making this move, later saying that it was a key moment, effectively ending the match. Black now threatens ...d5, liquidating the position, and

the following sequence is Nepom-niachtchi's only chance to keep the game and thus the match going.

18.♘hg4 ♘xg4 19.hxg4 d5!
20.d4!? The only way to exert pressure. **20...exd4 21.exd5 ♖e4!**
22.♕c2 ♖f4!

This is what Magnus had to evaluate when going 17...♖d8!. Black keeps d4 protected, and while 23.♖xd4 ♖xd4 24.cxd4 ♘xd5 is objectively White's best – with a draw, and if anyone will be able to exert pressure, it's Black – Nepomniachtchi plays what could be seen as the 'logical' move, as it forces Black's rook away from the protection of d4. However, the problem is that it loses trivially and instantly.
23.g3? dxe3! 24.gxf4

With his win in Game 11, Magnus Carlsen not only decided the match, but also turned his overall lifetime score against Ian Nepomniachtchi in classical chess into a 5-4 lead.

24...♕xg4+
Nepomniachtchi commented after the game that for some reason he had only expected 24...exf2+. It is hard to explain such an error, except because of tiredness and disillusion.
25.♔f1 ♕h3+ 26.♔g1

26...♘f5!
This move faced some criticism, and it is true that the evaluation dropped from like -11 to -7. There is a famous anecdote that at a team gathering during an Olympiad, Swedish legend Ulf Andersson, to the puzzlement of his team mates, said: 'In this position there is at least mate'. There is a reasonable point in saying that in an absolute form, mate is the ultimate goal of chess, but from a practical point of view, a completely winning endgame may be a much safer option. Sure, 26...exf2+ 27.♕xf2 (27.♔xf2 ♕h2+ wins the queen) 27...♖d6 28.♕f1 ♖g6+ 29.♔f2 ♕h2+ 30.♔f3 ♖g3+ 31.♔e4 ♕xb2 leads to a winning attack, with White being mated shortly. But the line looks somewhat abstract, and the probability of having mis-calculated something exists, while the game continuation is clear-cut and trivial. Celebrations might be an hour later, but it's professionalism not to take the slightest unnecessary risk.
27.d6 The only chance. If 27.fxe3 then ♖d6! wins trivially.

Nepomniachtchi's loss was historically bad

The 2021 World Championship match fizzled out as Ian Nepomniachtchi, the challenger for the title, collapsed in the last six games, losing by a final score of 0 wins, 4 losses and 7 draws. How bad was his performance? Based on the winning percentage of the champion, Magnus Carlsen, it was the most one-sided result since 1910 and the fourth worst in the history of the World Championship, as shown below.

DYLAN LOEB McCLAIN

YEAR	WINNER	LOSER	VICTOR'S WINNING PERCENTAGE (wins plus 1/2 of draws)	GAMES PLAYED / MAX
1886	Wilhelm Steinitz	Johannes Zukertort	62,5 %	20 / 10 wins
1894	Emanuel Lasker	Steinitz	63,2 %	19 / 10 wins
1896-97	Lasker	Steinitz	73,5 %	17 / 10 wins
1907	Lasker	Frank J. Marshall	76,7 %	15 / 8 wins
1908	Lasker	Siegbert Tarrasch	65,6 %	16 / 8 wins
1910	Lasker*	Carl Schlechter	50,0 %	10 / 10
1910	Lasker	Dawid Janowski	86,4 %	11 / 8 wins
1921	José Raul Capablanca	Lasker	64,3 %	14 / 24
1927	Alexander Alekhine	Capablanca	54,4 %	34 / 6 wins
1929	Alekhine	Efim Bogoljubov	62,0 %	25 / 6 wins and 15 points
1934	Alekhine	Bogoljubov	59,6 %	26 / 6 wins and 15 points
1935	Max Euwe	Alekhine	51,7 %	30 / 6 wins and 15 points
1937	Alekhine	Euwe	62,0 %	25 / 6 wins and 15 points
1951	Mikhail Botvinnik*	David Bronstein	50,0 %	24 / 24
1954	Botvinnik*	Vasily Smyslov	50,0 %	24 / 24
1957	Smyslov	Botvinnik	56,8 %	22 / 24
1958	Botvinnik	Smyslov	54,3 %	23 / 24
1960	Mikhail Tal	Botvinnik	59,5 %	21 / 24
1961	Botvinnik	Tal	61,9 %	21 / 24
1963	Tigran Petrosian	Botvinnik	56,8 %	22 / 24
1966	Petrosian	Boris Spassky	52,1 %	24 / 24
1969	Spassky	Petrosian	54,3 %	23 / 24
1972	Bobby Fischer	Spassky	59,5 % **	21 / 24
1974	Anatoly Karpov	Viktor Kortchnoi	52,1 %	24 / 24
1978	Karpov	Kortchnoi	51,6 %	32 / 6 wins
1981	Karpov	Kortchnoi	61,1 %	18 / 6 wins
1984-85	Karpov　NO WINNER	Garry Kasparov	52,1 % (Karpov was leading)	48 / 6 wins
1985	Kasparov	Karpov	54,2 %	24 / 24
1986	Kasparov	Karpov	52,1 %	24 / 24
1987	Kasparov*	Karpov	50,0 %	24 / 24
1990	Kasparov	Karpov	52,1 %	24 / 24
1993	Kasparov	Nigel Short	62,5 %	20 / 24
1993	Karpov	Jan Timman	59,5 %	21 / 24
1995	Kasparov	Viswanathan Anand	58,3 %	18 / 20
1996	Karpov	Gata Kamsky	58,3 %	18 / 20
2000	Vladimir Kramnik	Kasparov	56,7 %	15 / 16
2004	Kramnik*	Peter Leko	50,0 %	14 / 14
2006	Kramnik	Veselin Topalov	50,0 % **	12 / 12
2008	Anand	Kramnik	59,1 %	11 / 12
2010	Anand	Topalov	54,2 %	12 / 12
2012	Anand	Boris Gelfand	50,0 %	12 / 12
2013	Magnus Carlsen	Anand	65,0 %	10 / 12
2014	Carlsen	Anand	59,1 %	11 / 12
2016	Carlsen	Sergey Karjakin	50,0 %	12 / 12
2018	Carlsen	Fabiano Caruana	50,0 %	12 / 12
2021	Carlsen	Ian Nepomniachtchi	68,2 %	11 / 14

NOTE : The chart excludes the finals of the FIDE elimination tournaments of 1998, 2002 and 2004.

* The defending champion kept the title when the match ended in a tie and there was no playoff.

** Includes a forfeit loss by the winner.

Lasker and Janowski played a match in 1909, which Lasker won easily (80 %), but there is wide agreement that it was not a title match.

Lasker resigned the match before it was officially over.

Dawid Janowski suffered the most lopsided loss in World Championship history (0 wins, 8 losses, 3 draws).

The candidates final. Though it was not a match for the title, it ended up being a de facto one after Fischer later refused to play Karpov.

The match was controversially suspended after five months with no victor. FIDE then switched back to matches of limited duration.

Viswanathan Anand's loss in 2013 (0 wins, 3 losses, 7 draws) had been the worst in the modern era until Nepomniachtchi.

Period during which the World Championship was split between the classical and the FIDE titles.

RAPID PLAYOFFS (best of 4 games)

62,5 %

62,5 %

75,0 %

100 %

27...♘h4! 28.fxe3 ♕g3+ 29.♔f1 ♘f3 30.♕f2 ♕h3+ 31.♕g2 ♕xg2+ 32.♔xg2 ♘xe1+ 33.♖xe1 ♖xd6

This was the position Magnus had aimed for. Black has an extra pawn and the active rook. More than enough for an easy win.

34.♔f3 ♖d2 35.♖b1 g6!

A good and careful move. White's only chance is b4, and the more 'active' 35... f5, for example, would just create a black weakness in that scenario.

36.b4 axb4 37.♖xb4 ♖a2! 38.♔e4 h5! 39.♔d5

39...♖c2! Impeccable technique.

40.♖b3 h4 41.♔c6 h3 42.♔xc7 h2 43.♖b1

43...♖xc3+

43...f6, followed by ...g5, would lead to a race that Black would win easily, but once again Magnus chooses a more clinical solution.

44.♔xb6 ♖b3+! 45.♖xb3 h1♕ 46.a5 ♕e4 47.♔a7 ♕e7+ 48.♔a8

48...♔g7! Not falling for 48...♕d8+?? 49.♖b8!. **49.♖b6 ♕c5**

And here Ian Nepomniachtchi resigned and was the first to congratulate Magnus on his successful title defence.

The last 14 years of my working life have been focused on preparing for World Championship matches, first for Vishy Anand, then for Magnus Carlsen. With experience you realize that things will eventually come to a sudden end. In the seven World Championship matches that I have been part of, four times the match was tied before the final game. One can only begin to imagine the pressure the players must be under, knowing that a tiny mistake might cost them the title and what comes with it. But even as a second, it is impossible before such a game not to have the thought that today might be the last day that your boss plays for the title.

The match in Dubai was peculiar in the sense that we in the team knew that it was probably Magnus's last match, regardless of the result. It diffused and added pressure simultaneously. Not having to care about future matches was a relief, but of course, we wanted it to end on a high note. Working for players like Vishy and Magnus, who dominated their respective generations, one gets to understand that what defines dominance is the ability to win even when things do not work out the way they had been planned to. And Magnus had his share of such matches.

Before Dubai, we in the team really hoped that in this match Magnus would get a chance to show how strong a player he actually is. And if this was indeed Magnus's last World Championship match, something he has said himself, then rather than feeling disappointment, one should embrace what a unique performance it was, especially with Game 6 standing out as a titanic sporting achievement. On the other hand, I recall the conversation with Vishy after his surprising victory in the 2014 Candidates' tournament. Congratulating him, I dared to say that I thought he had played his last World Championship match already, getting the immediate witty reply: 'So did I'. And that just goes to show that the future is hard to predict.

∎ ∎ ∎

Aftermath

The final game was widely viewed as a kind of suicide, the event having become pointless and excruciating for the challenger. As the blunders escalated in scale – pawn, piece and finally king – it was very hard indeed not to feel that there was at least a subconscious desire to make the final result, and the final games, so anomalous that it would be easier to dismiss the match as an aberration and not reflective of any genuine difference in actual playing ability.

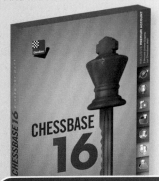 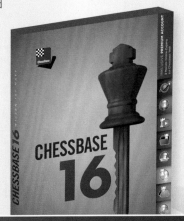

Indeed, Ian Nepomniachtchi's immediate framing of the result was to say, several times, that it had 'nothing – or little' – to do with chess, and he needed to understand how other factors – presumably linked to psychological issues like nerves, concentration or confidence – had influenced the result. This gradually evolved into: 'I think first of all what chess teaches you is the responsibility, because you are the one who is moving the pieces, you make the decisions and face the consequences.' Certainly, the result would not reflect badly on his seconds.

Carlsen summed up his success thus: 'In simple positions I make very few mistakes. A few times the position was very complicated, we both made mistakes, but he made the last one.' He left Dubai with a career plus score against his old chum and rival. As Carlsen said recently after beating troublesome Jan-Krzysztof Duda – 'I don't get revenge by beating people once!'

Reading minds

One of the most remarkable comments about the course of the contest came from esteemed GM and philosopher Jonathan Rowson, who pointed out that he had written precisely about unforced errors, and in regard to Magnus, particularly in matches.

From his latest book *The Moves that Matter*: 'The strong weaken the weaker because strength is ultimately a function of the will, and in a context where there is no escape, one side's will ultimately yield to the other ... The strength of really strong players lies precisely in their ability to make other strong players play below their strength.'

The final press conference. While Ian Nepomniachtchi clearly would have preferred to be somewhere else, Magnus Carlsen was fairly restrained after his fifth win in a World Championship match.

On a related note, I can't help observing that the exertion of the will in practice is not always a simple business. It is very easy to argue that Magnus's will to win was directly responsible for his reckless and near-fatal loss to Karjakin in 2016, and could of course have cost him dearly in Dubai. It entails risk. But besides them paying off well, Magnus is *completely* conscious about his decisions. Discussing Ian's history of cracking after setbacks, Magnus said: 'That's not something he can allow himself in a World Championship match. I am not going to fall, even if I am hit in the face once.'

When you are prepared to be hit in the face, you can lead with your face.

In search of giants

The fifth consecutive title match victory left the champion 'fully satisfied' with his performance for a change. The most telling quote from his victory speech was his thanks to his team: 'Even at a moment when my motivation may have been lacking for this particular championship, [my team's] motivation never wavered!' Magnus's reference to his own motivation is a familiar refrain, and in his last interview in Norway he hinted that this title defence could be his last. In a post-match podcast with chum Barstad, Magnus said he had enough of playing title matches, and currently only feels motivated to take on the next generation, namely, new world number two Alireza Firouzja, if the teenager can win the pressure-cooker Candidates event.

Magnus has always been sceptical about the demands of the classical title cycle, but this is a new level of disillusionment. So far, he has always changed his mind. Nothing grates more on a champion's mentality than giving away something won. It doesn't appear to hint at any thoughts of retirement, quite the reverse I believe.

Along with wanting only to face the best of the coming generation, Magnus has also announced a goal of breaking the 2900 rating barrier. Both of these have extreme implications, placing demands on himself that seem to me designed to rejuvenate and re-ignite his flagging motivation. He wants to reach inhuman heights, and fight those most likely – sooner or later – to dethrone him. Sounds worth watching. ∎

World Championship match Dubai 2021																				
				1	2	3	4	5	6	7	8	9	10	11	12	13	14		
Magnus Carlsen	IGM	NOR	2855	½	½	½	½	½	1	½	1	1	½	1	-	-	-	7½	2912
Ian Nepomniachtchi	IGM	RUS	2782	½	½	½	½	½	0	½	0	0	½	0	-	-	-	3½	2725

BLUNDER AND LOVE

OK, I admit it. I was a little happy Ian Nepomniachtchi made that blunder of the bishop in Game 9 of the World Championship. Not in a mean way. More in a selfish way. I don't know what it's like to be the second best in the world at anything. Anyone who thinks he knows what happened during the moments Ian made these blunders is an idiot.

It must be an enormous pleasure to be the second best in the world at... anything. How many people play chess on this planet? A billion? 80 million people are good enough to play online and a lot more have probably never played online but know the rules.

Imagine being #2 out of a billion people. For those weeks that he was playing Magnus Carlsen, and those months he was preparing, he was number two. And in his own head he might've been number one. Maybe that's how you go from being number two to number one. But I'll never know what that's like.

Still, though, I maybe know a little how he felt when he made those blunders. When he made a move that didn't feel like it was the real him. When something jammed up

Nepo made a move that felt like he was sabotaging his entire life and on the road to losing everything

his brain and he made a move that left him in a position where, if someone said, 'Black to move and win', he would've seen the answer in 1/20 a second. Where he made a move that felt like he was sabotaging his entire life and on the road to losing everything.

For instance, there were a few years where I used to day trade for a living. Some days I would make a trade and it would instantly go against me. Every tick of the market going against me I felt like I was vomiting out everything in my brain.

I was in misery looking at that screen. How could I have put on that trade? What was wrong with me? I'd leave the house and go across the street where there was a church. I'd kneel in front of the statue of Jesus and pray that by the time I returned home the market would be on my side again, would be my friend again and love me.

I'm Jewish so maybe it didn't make any sense to pray in a church. By the end of the day, down money, out of the trade, I was always afraid. What if every day was now like this. Only a few more months of trades like this and I'd go broke. It could happen. And I felt like I had no control over it. And every now and then, sometimes just a few months later. I would be broke and have to rebuild. Then the next day I'd start all over again.

I quit day trading because I couldn't handle all the emotions. Even when I was doing well. It's too up and down. I didn't play in chess tournaments for 25 years after hitting 2200 and now I'm starting to play again – maybe it's because I am now starting to handle these emotions. Or trying to.

Chess is a practice. It's a safe way to face the terror of life. When life is great, we claim to see every move to the bitter end. When life is not going our way, it's a 'blunder'. It's not the real me. 'How could I make that move? What's gotten into me?'

Look for checks, captures, threats, attacks. A checklist. Like Atul Gawande writes in *The Checklist Manifesto*, describing the technique he uses in the operating room. OK, I will. But I was following the checklist that last tournament and then for one move, one special move because I was winning that entire game, or I was drawing, or I should've been better, or the outcome should've been different if the world made sense – for that one moment I forgot the checklist and I blunder and lose. Ugh!!

I'm glad Ian Nepomniachtchi made those blunders because maybe it means there's nothing wrong with me. Blunders happen. 'What's happening to me?' has an answer. I've given up entire careers because of a blunder, but Ian said, 'There's a lot of work to do' to figure these blunders out.

He doesn't mean he has to figure out what the right moves were. He knows what they were. He knew them the second he made the blunder. What work does he have to do then? Does he have to practice calculation?

Of course not! The man can solve a 'mate in 6212 moves position'. Blunders don't come from the same part of the brain as tactics. This is important to know. Tactics and calculation belong to the logical reasoning part of the brain. The safe part. You can train that part of the brain. You can harness it and rein it in and teach it to work for you.

Blunders come from the part of the brain that's beyond reason. It's the part of the brain where you made a wrong turn somewhere and you got lost, and not only lost the way but forgot what the destination even was. Where dreams exist but the results are unknown and dark and hidden. Ian wants to figure out how to find his way out of that part of the brain when he needs to. How to find his destination again. How to continue through and find home.

Time, known for its medicinal ability in repairing lost love, also repairs blunders

There was a study at NYU which found that monkeys playing a computer game will slow down their decision making the next time they play a game after making a mistake. But... they still make 'Blunders' (paraphrasing). When similar tests were done on humans it's because our brain is filled with thoughts like, 'Is there something wrong with me?', so it adds negative information to the decision making process. But time heals that thought. Time, known for its medicinal ability in repairing lost love, also repairs blunders.

Ian was on stage to show us that the worst things in life can happen and often do. People often say, 'How do I stop blundering?' Now we know the answer. Now we have it. You can't stop blundering. Just accept it and that will start you on a path to improvement. You can, though, reduce blunders. Sure: check for the checks, look for captures, look for the intermediate moves and any double attacks and discovered attacks and skewered attacks. Look for them all every move.

In my podcast Judit Polgar recommended to me that I should practice blindfold chess. 'I did a lot of this as a little girl.' Cyrus Lakdawala, in a recent article, suggested studying endgame compositions. Axel Smith suggests the Woodpecker Method to get used to as many patterns as possible.

Sure, if you do all of these or any of these you will get better and you will blunder less. And for most players out there, the easiest way to gain several hundred rating

points is to just blunder less than your opponent. Chess is not simple but for most people it's just a matter of 'don't blunder before your opponent does' and that's how 98% of the world's chess games are decided.

But Ian blundered and lost the chance to be number one out of a billion people. An Emperor of the Mind! And I'm sure he felt everything in his life slip away for just a moment, maybe more.

But he went to the press conferences. He said, 'I have a lot of work to do' to figure out why he made those blunders. I guess he did some of that work, and kept going and he played in the World Blitz and Rapid (where he scored the same number of points as Carlsen, Caruana, and the new World Rapid Champion Abdusattorov – in other words, he tied for first).

What work, Ian? What work did he do? What's the secret training that a world #2 does to smooth out these calluses of the soul? Tell us!

Heck, you and I already know the answer. You need to forget about it the next day and work harder than everyone else.

Ding Liren vs Magnus Carlsen in the Magnus Carlsen Invitational 2020 (position after 31.♕d3)

According to the computer, Black (Magnus) is slightly better. Then Magnus makes the move 31...♔h7??. Number one. White to move and win. And no solution is provided.

James Altucher has written 25 books. About 21 of them are bad but one or two are OK. He has started several companies and has a popular podcast called 'The James Altucher Show'. Among others, Garry Kasparov and Judit Polgar have been guests on his podcast, as well as Kareem Abdul-Jabbar, Richard Branson and 963 others. He has played chess since he was 16 but stopped when he hit 2204 USCF in 1997, and is now starting to play again.

Where is the Silicon Road leading us?

The impact of the match in Dubai on modern professional *and* amateur chess

Magnus Carlsen and his father Henrik at the closing. The match in Dubai provided ample food for thought.

Magnus Carlsen's head trainer Peter Heine Nielsen called the clash in Dubai 'the first World Championship match in the era of neural networks'. **MATTHEW SADLER,** whose recent book *The Silicon Road to Chess Improvement* looks at the role of engines in today's chess (at all levels), was a fascinated spectator.

Back in October 2021, Daniil Dubov (one of Magnus Carlsen's seconds) suggested in an interview with chess.com that chess engines had improved as much in the past three years as in the fifteen years before. Gian-Carlo Pascutto – author of the strong Stoofvlees engine – pointed out that the data didn't support this, but I think that Dubov's assessment strikes a chord with professional players nonetheless. In 2017, I still fervently believed in my added creative value when analysing with an engine, particularly in two aspects: opening play and long-term planning/evaluation. In the opening engines lacked the urgency that humans have in that phase, an urgency arising from a sense of the logic of opening play and a feel for the fleeting opportunities that arise as both sides initiate their development.

This self-belief has fallen away completely in the last three years! More or less all of the top engines now use a self-learned evaluation – some like Leela Zero building on the legacy of AlphaZero, others like Stockfish using different technology – and this component has completely transformed their strength in these areas.

A nice example of this opening strength was seen in Game 1 of the match, where Magnus uncorked the unusual 8...♘a5 in the Anti-Marshall.

Ian Nepomniachtchi
Magnus Carlsen
Dubai 2021 (Game 1)
Ruy Lopez, Anti-Marshall

**1.e4 e5 2.♘f3 ♘c6 3.♗b5 a6
4.♗a4 ♘f6 5.0-0 ♗e7 6.♖e1 b5
7.♗b3 0-0 8.h3 ♘a5**

In an excellent ChessBase interview with Sagar Shah, Carlsen's head trainer Peter Heine Nielsen reacted laconically to praise of this move with 'You can turn on the computer, it won't say it's the best move but it will say it's there'.

And indeed the first game of the first engine match I ran from the position after 8...♘a5 between Komodo Dragon and Revenge (more on this later!) mirrored the Nepomniachtchi-Carlsen game until move 16!

Coming back to Dubov's suggestion, it may well be that the pace of engine improvement has not quickened, but in the past three years their improvement has encroached very heavily on the remaining areas where strong human players could still (occasionally) prove superior. Peter Heine put it very well when replying to a congratulatory tweet from Demis Hassabis (CEO of DeepMind, creator of AlphaZero): 'The first match in the era of neural networks, it has truly been a game changer. It enriched our understanding of the game like nothing before'.

Like nothing before

I might be giving the impression that modern preparation has become a matter of simply pointing a modern engine on powerful hardware at a position and waiting for an answer to pop out. In fact, I think the nature of creativity in preparation has changed in the engine age. In the 1990s (my era as a second), preparation started from a relative void, which you filled with inventive ideas and frantic all-night analysis. In the engine age, there is a mass of existing knowledge of a stratospherically high level and the possibility to generate much more at the press of a button. The creativity comes from translating 3600 Elo-level analysis (which is available to both players) to the struggle between two exceedingly strong but fallible 2800 Elo-level players. That might entail using move orders to trick your opponent into a structure he wasn't

The nature of creativity in preparation has changed in the engine age

aiming to play, or to exploit the opponent's desire to play one structure against everything.

Arguably, this is something Magnus did successfully in Game 2, where Ian was steered into a Dubov-style Catalan structure.

Magnus Carlsen
Ian Nepomniachtchi
Dubai 2021 (Game 2)
Catalan Opening, Open Variation

**1.d4 ♘f6 2.c4 e6 3.♘f3 d5
4.g3 ♗e7 5.♗g2 0-0 6.0-0 dxc4
7.♕c2 b5 8.♘e5 c6 9.a4**

And in Game 6, where Ian's determination to meet kingside fianchettoes with ...e6 and ....♗e7 was exploited to create this interesting opening line.

Magnus Carlsen
Ian Nepomniachtchi
Dubai 2021 (Game 6)
Queen's Pawn Opening (Pseudo-Catalan)

**1.d4 ♘f6 2.♘f3 d5 3.g3 e6 4.♗g2
♗e7 5.0-0 0-0 6.b3 c5 7.dxc5
♗xc5 8.c4 dxc4 9.♕c2 ♕e7
10.♘bd2**

This creativity also entails avoiding the top engine lines – which are surely known to both players – and opting for secondary lines that might have been overlooked or underestimated by the opponent.

An interesting example of this 'shadow battle' was in Game 3, after Black's 13th move:

Ian Nepomniachtchi
Magnus Carlsen
Dubai 2021 (Game 3)

position after 13...♘e7

Here, commentators such as Vishy Anand and Anish Giri spotted the aggressive idea of 14.g4 immedi-

Besides human help from his girlfriend Snezhana Fomicheva, his head trainer Vladimir Potkin and a big team of GMs (including Sergey Karjakin), Ian Nepomniachtchi may also have relied on the Zhores supercomputer to create a 'new brain' for Leela.

ately and it was also Leela's top move. When asked about this possibility, Peter Heine said that 'we wouldn't be doing our job properly if we hadn't analysed this', which I'm assuming means they had analysed this thoroughly!

Ian's second Vladimir Potkin – also interviewed on ChessBase by Sagar Shah – seemed to say that this move was known to them, but it was difficult to commit to it, unless you knew the opponent was going to play it. And in any case, the assumption was that Magnus would be prepared for it. With this background, you understand Ian's choice of 14.c4 better: a less critical move, lower in the engine listings and thus might have been missed by the opposing team, but with more than a little venom. As it turned out, Magnus found some excellent regroupings – possibly (half-)remembered from preparation – and neutralised the idea.

A 'new brain' for Leela

Peter Heine's tweet about this being the first match in the era of neural networks applied to the teams... and even to the spectators! Before the match we learned that Nepomniachtchi's team had access to the Russian Zhores supercomputer. Since it was built to aid scientific discoveries

Nepomniachtchi's team had access to the Russian Zhores supercomputer

in – amongst other things – machine learning, it raised some interesting possibilities. Using it just to analyse positions seemed a bit like overkill, but presumably Ian's team gained access both to the hardware itself and to scientific expertise so it would have been possible for them to create a new neural net (a 'new brain') for Leela

that might possibly find different moves to the nets generally available.

From the spectator point of view, during the match, the Leela developers were running tests (streamed on the www.twitch.tv/navratil25 website) with new 'heavier' (more complex) Leela neural nets. This 'big Leela' was kibitzing for part of the match and I also used it to analyse the games.

The Norwegian Sesse computer (analysis.sesse.net), which always follows Magnus' games, got a massive hardware upgrade and provided deep Stockfish analysis throughout the match.

After the match, I was involved in an interesting experiment together with the TCEC website, in which Stockfish, Leela Zero and Komodo Dragon played out critical positions from games in the match (the 42 games played are available here: tcec-chess.com/#div=wccb&game=1&season=21).

This way of analysing with engines is something I describe at length in *The Silicon Road to Chess Improvement* and I first got really keen on it after playing through hundreds of

AlphaZero-Stockfish QGD games. The contrasting plans and assessments of two radically different engines were easy to visualise and I learnt – and remembered – more from half an hour playing through glorious, evocative games than through a couple of hours staring at an engine screen with glazed eyes pressing the spacebar! Once Leela Zero landed on our laptops, it was easy to generate all the games you wanted on your own laptop!

It's beautiful for opening preparation and it's also a great way of feeling the flow of human games. An engine evaluation of +1.5 doesn't give you any understanding of the type of advantage or the difficulty in realising it; see a few games from your engines and you know exactly how things stand!

Let's look at a few examples to see what I mean.

Game 6 was the game of the match, with two crucial moments for Nepomniachtchi where he could have captured the b4-pawn (on moves 35 and 36) but elected instead to improve his position. From the engine games it was clear that 35...♗xb4 was not a big chance in principle, with both games drawn, and Stockfish even finding a concrete drawing path.

It seems that Ian's practical decision to increase the pressure with 35...e5 was justified but 36...♗xb4 was definitely a very serious chance. Leela was unable to hold White's position while Stockfish managed, but it was anything but easy!

Stockfish (3628)
Leela Zero (3609)
TCEC Season 21 – WCC2021
Bonus tcec-chess.com 2021 (18)

Carlsen-Nepomniachtchi
Game 6, position after 36.♖c2

36...♗xb4 37.♖cc1 ♗a3 38.♖a1 ♕g4

This was presumably the key tactical idea that Ian missed when considering 36...♗xb4. It's the only way for Black to protect the bishop while keeping all of his pawns.
39.♖d2 ♗e7 40.♘e1 ♔h7 41.♖da2 a3 42.♔g1 ♕c8 43.♔h2 f5 44.♘f3 ♕c3 45.♘g1 ♗b4 46.♘e2

This was basically Stockfish's defensive structure, which it held until move 117, when Leela engineered the ...f4 break.

position after 117...f4

118.exf4 exf4 119.♘e2 fxg3+ 120.fxg3 ♔a4 121.♘f4 ♕f3 122.♖g1 ♗d6 123.♖gg2 ♕e4 124.♖ae2 ♕c4 125.♖gf2

And this new defensive structure proved enough to hold until the 178th move, when the draw was agreed!

Amazing resistance

Game 8 featured a bad mistake from Ian (21...b5) after which Magnus won a pawn and finished smoothly with impeccable technique. I had quickly dismissed Ian's position as

hopeless after 21...b5 so I was amazed at the resistance that the engines managed to put up. Leela was unable to convert against Komodo Dragon and Komodo Dragon needed some wonderful technique to put Leela away.

Komodo Dragon (3591)
Leela Zero (3609)
TCEC Season 21 – WCC2021
Bonus tcec-chess.com 2021 (19)

Carlsen-Nepomniachtchi
Game 8, position after 22.♕a3

22...♕d6 23.♕xa7 g5 24.♗d3 ♔g7 25.a4 bxa4 26.♖e5 f6 27.♖e2 ♖h8 28.♕xa4 ♖e8 29.♖xe8 ♗xe8 30.♕a7+ ♕d7 31.♕xd7+ ♗xd7

When he saw this playout, Anish Giri tweeted that he would consider it an acceptable result after blundering a pawn which is a good way to look at it I think. The conversion is certainly not easy: **32.♔f1 ♔f7 33.♔e2 ♔e6 34.♔e3 ♔d5 35.♗e2 ♗e6 36.♗g4 f5 37.♗f3+ ♔d6 38.b4 ♗c8 39.♗d1 ♗e6 40.♗c2 ♗d5 41.f3 f4+ 42.♔d3 ♗e6 43.♔c3 ♗c8 44.♗g6 ♗d7 45.♔d3**

♔e7 46.♗h7 ♗e6 47.♔c3 ♔d6 48.♗d3 ♗c8 49.♗c4 ♗f5 50.♗b3 ♗g6 51.♔a4 ♗d7 52.♔a5 ♗h7 53.♔b6 ♔d6 54.♔a7 ♗g6

55.d5 ♗f7 55...cxd5 56.♗e2 and the b-pawn cannot be stopped!
56.♔b6 cxd5 57.♗d3 d4 58.♔a7
A lovely sequence! The king moves back to a7 to shepherd the b-pawn home!
58...♗e8 59.b5 ♔c5 60.b6 ♗c6 61.b7 ♗xb7 62.♔xb7 ♔b4 63.♔c6 ♔c3 64.♔b5 ♔d2 65.♔d5 ♔e3 66.♔e5 ♔f2 67.♔f5
And White won on the 80th move.

A crucial moment

Game 2 was also a crucial moment in the match. It felt as if Magnus had lost his way in the intricacies of his own preparation and that Ian had an advantage in the irrational type of position that should suit him. However, as the engines demonstrated, the win was far from easy and only Stockfish demonstrated a clear path through the complications.

Leela Zero (3609)
Stockfish (3628)
TCEC Season 21 – WCC2021
Bonus tcec-chess.com 2021 (27)

Carlsen-Nepomniachtchi
Game 2, position after 23.♖d1

Here **23...bxa4** was the unanimous choice of my engines, instead of Ian's 23...♗a8, and after **24.♗e4** then **24...g6** was a very important move. 24...♗c8 was both Leela's and Komodo's choice, but the amazing 25.♗xh7+ ♔xh7 26.♕h5+ ♔g8 27.♖d4 ♕d8 28.♖h4 ♕xh4 29.gxh4 c3 30.bxc3 a3 31.♘xc8 ♖bxc8 32.♕g4 ♖b8 33.♕a4 ♖b1+ 34.♔g2 ♖b2 35.♕xa3 fxf2+ 36.♔g3 held for White in both matchups between these engines.
25.♕xc4 c5 26.♖d2 ♗xe4 27.♘xe4 ♕c6 28.♖d6 ♕c8 29.♘f6+ ♔h8

This position looks very scary for Black – I would be continually worrying I was losing in a practical game – but it's basically as good as it gets for White.
30.♕xa4 ♖xb2 31.♕xa7 ♖b7 32.♕a3 g5 33.♕c3 c4 34.♔g2 ♕a8 35.♔h3 ♖c7 36.f3 ♕b7

The rook on the second rank covers h7 and supports the c-pawn, while the black queen is free to harass the white king and try to force the white queen from c3. For engines, Black is now easily winning.

MAYBE YOU NEED SOME DISTRACTION, DARLING...

WHY DON'T YOU TAKE UP A HOBBY?

BEREND VONK

37.g4 ♕b1 38.♔g2 ♖a7 39.♖d2
♖a2 40.♖xa2 ♕xa2+ 41.♔g3
♕e2 42.♕d4 h5 43.gxh5 ♕e1+
44.♔g2 c3 45.♕a7 ♕e2+
46.♔g1 ♕d1+ 47.♔g2 ♕c2+
48.♔g3 ♕f5 49.♔f2 ♖d8 50.♘e4
g4 51.♕e3 ♕xh5 52.♕xc3
♕xh2+ 53.♔e3 g3 54.♕c7
♕g1+ 55.♔f4 ♖f8+ 56.♘f6 ♕h2
57.♕e7 g2+ 58.♔e4 ♕h4+
59.♔d3 ♖c8 60.♕f8+ ♖xf8 61.f4
g1♕ 62.♘e4 ♕xf4 63.♔c4
♕xe4+ 64.♔b3 ♖b8+ 65.♔a3
♕a8 Mate.

Relatively minimal discomfort

Finally, Game 9 will forever be remembered for Ian's tragic blunder, but there were some uncertain moments in the opening which the engine games helped to resolve. After 14...a3, Ian's 15.bxa3 led nowhere, but 15.b4 was the top engine move and widely recommended after the game. However, the engine games showed that Black's discomfort was relatively minimal – certainly for a World Championship game!

Stockfish (3628)
Leela Zero (3609)
TCEC Season 21 – WCC2021
Bonus tcec-chess.com 2021 (24)

Nepomniachtchi-Carlsen
Game 9, position after 14...a3

15.b4
This critical move requires some accurate calculation from Black.
15...♘xb4 16.♖b1 b6 17.♖xb4 bxc5 18.♖b5 ♖a6
The key idea. 18...cxd4 19.♘xd4 hits a8 and g4.

Such clear insights never arrived so quickly after a World Championship match – yet another consequence of living in the era of neural nets!

19.♖xc5 ♗b7 20.♕b1 ♗a8

Black has managed to get all the pieces developed and held the engine games comfortably.
**21.h3 ♘f6 22.♘e5 ♗xg2
23.♔xg2 ♕d8 24.♘f3 h6 25.♖b5
♕a8 26.♕d3 ♖d8 27.♖fb1 ♕e4
28.♕xe4 ♘xe4 29.♖e1 ♘g5** And the game was drawn in 54 moves.

All-in-all, I felt that such clear insights had never arrived so quickly after a World Championship match – yet another consequence of living in the era of neural nets!

What's next?

Just to round off, while chatting on the TCEC website, I got into some discussions about the things you could do if you looked at the World Championship as an enterprise IT project, a topic which intrigued me as an IT professional by day (I'm a Solution Architect for a French IT company).

For example, Magnus' team has been working on World Championships

since 2013. They prepared the Anti-Marshall against Sergey Karjakin in 2016 so they have a huge amount of historical analysis to manage, supplemented by vast amounts of recent analysis by teams working remotely. It sounds strikingly like a modern software development project: you need to merge recent work from different teams all over the world, maintain good versioning, be able to roll back bad analysis and have a clear picture at all times of what the main lines actually are. That's not trivial to do in a standard tool like Chess-Base, so you do wonder whether these teams got some custom software built to better manage the huge volume of analysis that they have.

Also, one of the holy grails of enterprise IT is automation. Thinking about the work of seconds, a lot of time must be spent manually ploughing through databases/ analysis trying to find/generate promising ideas. It would seem possible to create a tool that works through opening databases, analysing positions with multiple, stylistically different engines like Stockfish and Leela (for multiple viewpoints), automatically flagging up significant differences in evaluation (which would be a promising starting point for investigation) and presenting a list of possible avenues for a second to explore further.

Interestingly, the basis of this already exists at chessdb.cn which I consulted frequently during the match. It's an opening database entirely built up from engine (Stockfish) analysis with no human input and you frequently saw Ian's and Magnus' choices high up in its list of moves!

That's perhaps the only reason to look forward to Magnus retiring: so that Peter Heine Nielsen can write the definitive book of recent World Championship history and that we will really know what the teams came up with! ■

When Patti met Bobby

Did Bobby Fischer really sing with the godmother of punk?

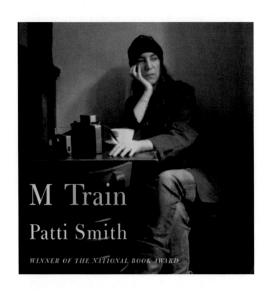

With their New York background and their shared passion for music, Patti Smith and Bobby Fischer no doubt had a lot to talk about. But how truthful is Smith's account in her memoir *M Train* of the encounter she had with the chess champion when he was living in exile in Reykjavik? **DIRK JAN TEN GEUZENDAM** harbours serious doubts.

She has been called 'the godmother of punk' and 'the punk poet laureate'. Patti Smith (b.1946) is an iconic pop artist, whose debut album *Horses* is as alive today as it was in 1975. The album is a classic, as is the black and white cover photo shot by Robert Mapplethorpe, imagining Smith as a latter-day Baudelaire. She's a poet herself, a visual artist and also an acclaimed writer. Her book *Just Kids* (2010), about her relationship with Mapplethorpe, won the National Book Award and continues to be a bestseller.

In 2015 Patti Smith published another memoir, *M Train*, with the M standing for memory. Memories of Greenwich Village, where she starts the book drinking black coffee in a café, and memories of travels and people she met around the world. One of those meetings is with Bobby Fischer, during his final years in Iceland.

Given the attention the encounter with the former chess champion received in the reviews of the book and in the interviews Smith gave when it appeared, the space that she actually dedicates to Fischer is a bit disappointing. She arrives in Iceland at the bottom of page 39, and less than four pages further on the meeting is over. Still, in those few pages she gives details that the reader will not easily forget. And will believe to be true.

On the book's dust-jacket, Patti Smith's prose is described as '[shifting] fluidly between dreams and reality, past and present, and across a landscape of creative aspirations and inspirations'. If you have read the book, you may wonder how far a writer is allowed to drift from reality.

Smith writes that she was in Iceland in 2007 for a meeting of the Continental Drift Club, an obscure society of only 27 members worldwide. They are all fascinated by Alfred Wegener (1880-1930), a German meteorologist, geologist and polar explorer, who was the first to come up with the theory of the shifting continents. Smith became a member (long story short) when she sent the Alfred Wegener Institute in Bremerhaven a request to photograph the boots of the legendary explorer.

Because she is also an avid photographer.

Her plans in Iceland dramatically shift from Alfred Wegener to chess when a fellow member of the Continental Drift Club, 'a thoroughly robust Icelandic grandmaster', tells her that he has been invited to an expedition to Greenland. He'd love to go, but he has committed himself to handing out prizes at a children's chess tournament. If she could do that for him, he has a very special reward for her in return: he'd arrange for her to photograph the table used in the 1972 chess match between Bobby Fischer and Boris Spassky, 'currently languishing in the basement of a local government facility'.

The opportunity to photograph 'the holy grail' of chess is too attractive for the photographer Smith and she turns up at the children's tournament where the table is 'unceremoniously delivered'. What's more, she is not the only photographer around and, as she writes, the next day the picture of her at the fabled table 'graced the cover of the morning newspaper.'

And there was more chess in store for her. First, having photographed the chess table, she spends the afternoon with a friend in the countryside riding 'sturdy Icelandic ponies'. Then, on her return, she receives a call from a man 'identifying himself as Bobby Fischer's bodyguard'. He has been asked to arrange a meeting between 'Mr. Fischer' and her in the closed dining room of Hotel Borg. That is the hotel where she is staying and, incidentally, was the hotel where Bobby Fischer stayed when he visited Iceland for the first time in 1960 (and changed rooms three times). She is to bring her own bodyguard and is not

She gives details that the reader will not easily forget. And will believe to be true

permitted to bring up the subject of chess. She consents to the meeting.

Now, before we move on to the meeting between Patti Smith and Bobby Fischer, which lasts one page in the book, it might be a good idea to check if the photo that she described of her sitting at the most famous chess table of all time did really appear on the front page of an Icelandic newspaper. The answer is a firm yes. On Tuesday, 6 September 2005, a big photo graced the front page of *Morgunbladid*. Inside the paper there was another, rather similar photo of Patti Smith at the table with her camera in her hand. The accompanying article informs the reader that she not only handed out prizes to the

young chess players, but was also made an honorary member of the chess club Hrokurinn.

The photo was taken in the Culture House Museum in Reykjavik, and the table did not have to be carried up from the basement. It was kept in a small room in the Culture House after it had been shown there in an exhibition to celebrate the 30th anniversary of the match. Later it was transferred to the Icelandic National Museum where it is exhibited these days.

A further discrepancy in Smith's account is that all this did not take place in 2007, as she writes in her book, but in 2005 as the *Morgunbladid* archives show us. A forgivable error, as she was in Iceland

The photo of Patti Smith, camera in hand, seated at the table of the 1972 Fischer-Spassky match, that appeared on the front page of *Morgunbladid*.

many times. What is more difficult to fathom is why she doesn't say she was there for a concert and instead puts great emphasis on the Continental Drift Club meeting.

The concert she gave in 2005 was on the day she met Bobby Fischer and was reviewed in *Morgunbladid* two days later, on 8 September. Did she really have the time and the energy to go pony riding in the afternoon before the concert?

It is no longer a secret that Fischer's 'bodyguard' was none other than Icelandic grandmaster Helgi Olafsson, who described the misunderstanding in *Bobby Fischer Comes Home* (New In Chess, 2012) and didn't bother to explain to Patti Smith who he really was. In his book, Olafsson's description of the meeting is not much longer than one page either, yet the differences in tone and facts are remarkable, to put it mildly.

In *M Train*, Smith paints an ominous and tense atmosphere as Fischer arrives. He is wearing a hooded parka and doesn't bare his head for the first few minutes. Instead, 'he began testing me immediately by issuing a string of obscene and racially repellent references that morphed into

'Throughout the night we must have sung hundreds of songs'

paranoiac conspiracy rants.' She tells him he is wasting his time, and he sits staring at her silently.

Then, all of a sudden, everything changes. Fischer drops his hood and asks her if she knows any Buddy Holly songs. 'For the next few hours we were singing songs.' At one point, when Fischer 'attempted a chorus of "Big Girls Don't Cry" in falsetto', the 'bodyguard', who was waiting outside, burst in to see if everything was all right, and his boss reassures him that there is nothing to worry about; he was just singing.

According to Patti Smith, Bobby Fischer left 'just before first light'. She remains until the servers arrived to prepare the breakfast buffet. This is how she ends the chapter: 'It occurred to me, as the heavy curtains were opened and the morning light flooded the small dining area, that without a

doubt we sometimes eclipse our own dreams with reality.'

The stories of the meeting as Patti Smith and Helgi Olafsson wrote them down, differ materially, but their versions do not necessarily exclude each other. Nevertheless, it did feel strange that Olafsson did not even mention that they had been singing together. Had he witnessed a historical moment and not realized its significance? Looking for an answer, I decided to call him and clarify the matter. Olafsson's reaction when we spoke on the phone was unequivocal: there had not been any singing – not a single song.

What's more: 'There was no other "bodyguard" either, Patti was alone. And there was no condition that chess was not to be mentioned. And I never called her. I received a call from the Icelandic concert promoter, who told me that she'd like to meet Bobby Fischer. Bobby asked me to come along, which he regularly did, and I met Patti in the dining room of Hotel Borg. There were a few other guests, but it was a very quiet evening. Bobby arrived around a quarter past ten. I wanted to leave, but they both insisted that I stay and sit with them – which I did, but I just listened to them and didn't join the conversation. Bobby didn't say anything that could cause offence. He was very polite, almost shy. Actually, I was quite proud of him. And no, he didn't wear a hooded parka, he wore a leather jacket and a leather cap, one that I think (his wife) Miyoko had bought for him. They talked a lot about music. At some point, Patti said she always knew that he was into music.'

But no singing? Perhaps Fischer stayed on after Olafsson had left and they sang then? 'No, I drove him home. They talked for something like two hours. The atmosphere was very cordial, and as we walked out of Hotel Borg, Bobby said to Patti that it had been good to meet someone

Patti Smith and interviewer Jeffrey Browne of PBS News Hour, talking about her meeting with Bobby Fischer. 'Well, that's an absolutely true story.'

from the US. Patti was very kind, but it was also clear that she was tired after the concert. I really don't understand why she made up these stories afterwards.'

Passages from both *M Train* and *Bobby Fischer Comes Home* are included in John Donaldson's monumental *Bobby Fischer and His World* (Siles Press, 2020). The excerpts do not contradict each other, and are given without much comment among a huge number of other accounts written by people who met Bobby Fischer over the years.

Donaldson also includes a fragment from an interview Patti Smith gave to promote her book in 2015 to Jeffrey Browne of *PBS News Hour*, in which she says: 'Bobby just loved rock 'n roll, just loved it, since a boy... We spent till dawn singing songs – everything: the Chi-Lites, the Four Tops, Chuck Berry, Darlene Love, all these old songs.'

And when Fischer died in 2008, her thoughts again went back to these songs: 'I met with him in Iceland at midnight in a dark corner of an empty dining hall. Our designated bodyguards were appointed to stand vigil outside. We were not to speak of chess.

What we did speak of, until dawn, was rock 'n roll. (..) Throughout the night we must have sung hundreds of songs.'

Hundreds, that's a lot.

Watching the News Hour interview online, there was one thing that struck me in particular. When Jeffrey Browne says that amid the many amazing stories in *M Train* is the evening she met Bobby Fischer, Patti Smith immediately, without a second thought, replies: 'Well, that's an absolutely true story.'

Now, why did she say that? ∎

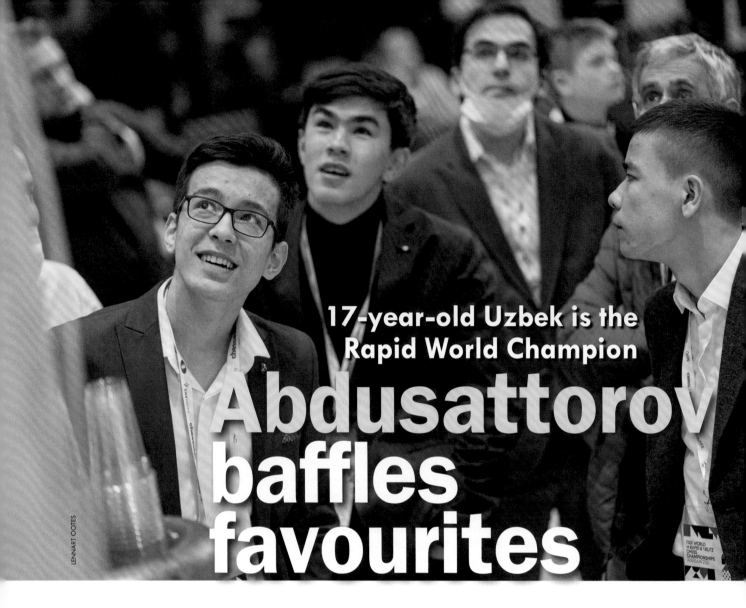

17-year-old Uzbek is the Rapid World Champion

Abdusattorov baffles favourites

Neither travel complications due to Covid, nor family duties, nor a last-minute change of venue could keep a formidable field of stars from flocking to Warsaw for the World Rapid & Blitz between Christmas and New Year. All eyes were on Carlsen, Nepomniachtchi, Duda, Caruana and the other usual suspects when the Rapid started, but they all had to bow to a young man no one had counted on: Nodirbek Abdusattorov. **ERWIN L'AMI** reports.

On December 8th, FIDE announced that the World Rapid and Blitz, scheduled to be held in Kazakhstan, was cancelled due to 'new covid restrictions' imposed in the country. With the rapid tournament set to start a mere 18 days later, I was impressed that a new venue was found in time. As a result, the championship was moved 4000 kilometres westwards, from the capital of Kazakhstan, Nur-Sultan (formerly Astana), to the capital of Poland, Warsaw. There, the National Stadium, normally host to Poland's national football team or concerts of famous stars, was transformed into the centre of the chess world for the days between Christmas and New Year. Since I did not set foot in the

Hikaru Nakamura
Vladimir Fedoseev
Warsaw World Rapid 2021 (9)

position after 27...♘b3

Black's last move intends to win the
b4-pawn. Hikaru is quick to spot a tactic.

28.♖xe6! fxe6

Since 28...♖xe6 29.♕f4! hits the b8-rook
and prepares ♗c4 and ♘f5. There is no
way to defend against all these threats.
The move Fedoseev plays is not the best
solution either. However, the saving
line 28...♕xh4+ 29.gxh4 ♘xd2 30.♖e2
♘f1+! (30...♘b3 31.♖e4 may just be lost)
31.♔g1 ♖d8! is impossible to find in a
rapid game.

29.♕c2

The point! White simultaneously
attacks the knight on b3 and threatens
to infiltrate on c7, both targeting the
rook on b8 and threatening the king on
g8. Hikaru thrives when it comes to this
type of tactics.

29...♖xb4 The only way to stay in
the game was 29...♘d4 30.♕c7 ♖d8,
when a direct knock-out blow is not
apparent, but 31.♕h7+ ♔f8 32.♘g6+
♔e8 33.♗e4! keeps the black position
in a strong grip.

30.♕c8+ ♔g7 31.♕c7+

Nodirbek Abdusattorov

Born 8 September 2004 in Tashkent,
Uzbekistan

Career highlights:

2011 Wins U-8 division World Youth
Championship in Maribor,
Slovenia

2014 At 9 years old defeats two GMs,
Andrey Zhigalko and Rustam
Khusnutdinov, in Agzamov
Memorial, Tashkent

2015 At the age of 11, youngest
player ever to enter top 100
Juniors

2018 Grandmaster at the age of 13
years, 1 month and 11 days.
The second youngest in history at
the time.

2021 Wins first group of PNWCC
Super G60 on chess.com

2021 Second place in Tolstoy Cup,
Yasnaya Polyana, Russia, behind
Anish Giri

2021 Wins El Llobregat Open in Spain

2021 Wins Sitges Open in Barcelona,
Spain

2021 Wins Rapid World Championship
in Warsaw, Poland

31.♘g6!? would have been sufficient
as well, introducing the deadly threat
of ♕h8+.

31...♕f7 Or 31...♔g8 32.♗h7+ ♔f8
33.♘g6+ ♔e8 34.♕c8+, with mate in
two to follow.

---

tournament hall myself (because
I was following the action from
home), I cannot say much about the
playing conditions, but judging by the
tweets that Maxime Vachier-Lagrave
sent out, not everything was running
smoothly. In defence of the organizers, it must be said that pulling off
an event of this magnitude within two
weeks is quite a feat.

The usual suspects gathered in
Warsaw, with Magnus Carlsen as the
big favourite and, apart from Wesley
So and Ding Liren, the entire world's
top 10 present. With such an abun-

Pulling off an event of this magnitude within two weeks was quite a feat

dance of stars, it is hard to focus
on all players, but I did pay special
attention to some of them. To begin
with, I was curious how Ian Nepomniachtchi would do after his dramatic
World Championship match against
Carlsen. It takes a strong character to
come back from such an experience.

Another person that not only I, but
most of the chess world was paying
extra attention to was our streaming
ambassador Hikaru Nakamura.
Hikaru had not played on the board
for ages, but with his daily blitz
regimen he remains a fierce compet-
itor, as he had showed in the online
Speed Chess Championship and the
Magnus Carlsen Tour. I found the
following game vintage Hikaru.

32.♕c3+ ♖d4 33.♕xb3

Technically speaking, the material
is still equal, but White's pieces are
working well together and, more
importantly, the king on h2 is very
safe compared to the one on g7.
**33...♕xf2 34.♕xe6 ♖xd3
35.♕g6+ ♔f8 36.♕xh6+ ♔e7
37.♕h7+ ♔d6 38.♕xd3+**

And White won quickly (1-0, 52).

Playing on a real board is different
from handling your mouse, and
I honestly had not expected the
transition to be this smooth for
Nakamura. Not losing a single
game in the Rapid championship,
and scoring +5, can obviously only
be considered a fine result. In the
ensuing Blitz event, however, Hikaru
seemed a bit out of sorts on the first
day, and the positive Covid test that
followed the next day explained a lot.
It meant that Naka had to withdraw,
which was obviously a blow, and not
only for him. Seemingly unfazed,
Hikaru resumed his streaming career
from the hotel in Warsaw where he
was self-isolating for two weeks(!), so
I trust he will be fine again soon!

The best thing we have

After winning the World Championship match, Magnus Carlsen
hinted at the possibility that he
would not defend his title in the
future, unless the challenger's name
was Alireza Firouzja. I sincerely
hope that Magnus was merely disap-
pointed with the match against
Nepomniachtchi, a sentiment that
is commonly shared. However, for
Carlsen to be leaving the World
Championship cycle would be a giant
blow to the best thing we have in the
chess world. There is simply no other
chess event that comes even close
to gathering this amount of interest
from all over the world.

After this small note in parentheses,
let's talk about the man Magnus
mentioned: Alireza Firouzja. In the
wake of Magnus's statement, expec-
tations about Alireza – who recently
pushed his classical rating over
2800 and is now the number two
in the world – were obviously high.
As you will read elsewhere in this
issue, Alireza certainly delivered in
the Blitz, but in the Rapid section he
failed to play a big role. The following
clash in Round 7 was obviously
highly anticipated.

**Magnus Carlsen
Alireza Firouzja**
Warsaw World Rapid 2021 (7)

position after 33.♕d3

A rather nervy middlegame had led
to this position. With his last move,
Magnus prepares a bishop exchange
on a3 that would be very desirable from a strategic point of view.

It has the downside, however, of allowing 33...♗xe5 34.dxe5 g5!, and although the engine still believes this is playable, I doubt that many humans would be happy here with White, seeing that ...♘g6 is on the cards. Alireza pulled the trigger immediately.

33...g5 34.♘g4!

Black must have missed this major trend-shift. The check on h6 forces his next move.

34...♔g7 35.♘e3 ♖f7 36.f5

Intending to exchange pawns and gain the f5-square for the knight. Black is still fine at this point, but only for concrete reasons; strategically the position has become suspect.

36...♕d7

36...g4!? is a fun resource, whose point becomes clear after 37.hxg4? ♕h4+!. Instead, 37.♘xg4 ♖xf5 leads to approximately equal play. There is nothing wrong with the game continuation, though.

37.♖f1

37...h6 This was Black's last chance to stay in the game. As I wrote earlier, Black is in strategic danger but the 'sudden' attack' 37...♕c7 is not so easy to meet. Pawn g3 is hanging, and moving the knight allows Black to take on f5. Last but not least, 38.♖f3 ♘g6! brings in the cavalry.

38.♔g2

With the tactics out of the way, Black is busted, and knowing this full well, Alireza is incapable of putting up much resistance.

38...♔g8 39.♘g4

Immediately decisive.

39...♔g7 40.f6+ ♔h8 41.♘xh6 ♖h7 42.♘g4 ♕e8 43.♗a3

Nice technique – exchanging his worst piece.

43...♗xa3 44.♕xa3 ♕c8 45.♖c1 ♕e8 46.♘e5 ♔g8 47.♕f3 ♕d8 48.♖f1 ♔h8 49.♕e3 ♕c8 50.♖f2 g4 51.h4 ♖h5 52.♘f7+ ♔g8 53.♘g5 1-0.

Carlsen seemed to be cruising after this victory, and even more so after an important victory two rounds later against local hero Jan-Krzysztof Duda. In Round 10, the top-seed faced 17-year-old Nodirbek Abdusattorov from Uzbekistan. Not exactly a household name just yet, but he soon will be. I knew Nodirbek from when I played him in Wijk aan Zee in 2020, when he mixed something up in the opening and landed in deep trouble. I was truly impressed by his composure and tenacity as he eventually held a difficult endgame to a draw after 104 moves. I remember his fellow-countryman Rustam Kasimdzhanov, who knew Abdusattorov well, telling me that 'this kid is serious'.

In their game, Magnus was quietly outplaying Abdusattorov, but the latter bluntly refused to collapse. Defending tenaciously, the youngster managed to steer the game into equal waters, where the wisest thing for Carlsen would have been to take things to their natural outcome. The moment Magnus tried too hard to play for a win, his persistence backfired. Here is that dramatic game, with notes by Anish Giri.

NOTES BY
Anish Giri

Nodirbek Abdusattorov
Magnus Carlsen
Warsaw World Rapid 2021 (10)
English Opening, Four Knights Variation

1.c4 ♘f6 2.♘c3 e5 3.♘f3 ♘c6
4.e4 Nodirbek Abdusattorov had apparently prepared this system for this event. He used it very successfully, not only in this game, but also in the crucial tie-break match vs. Nepomniachtchi.
4...♗b4 The alternative 4...♗c5 leads to a mess after the 5.♘xe5!, as was seen in Carlsen-Giri in the same championship two years ago.
5.d3 d6

6.a3 Abdusattorov, but also other players alongside him, have tried 6.♗e2 and 6.h3 as well. These lead to slightly different lines, but conceptually they are all part of the same family of closed positions.
6...♗c5 Taking on c3 should not be too bad either, but everybody retreats nowadays.
7.b4 ♗b6 8.♘a4 ♗g4 Natural. In a closed position, Black is ready to give up the bishops for the knights. The alternative is 8...♘d4!?, which is more sophisticated, yet more common.
9.♘xb6 axb6 10.♗b2 ♗xf3
Capturing without provocation seems odd, but Black argues that the queen on f3 is misplaced and wants to capture before White goes ♗e2.
11.♕xf3 ♘d7 The knight is now likely to head towards e6, from where it will reinforce the control of the

d4-square. At this point it is very hard to say whether the bishops or the knights will prevail.
12.g3

Intending a fianchetto, or perhaps ♗h3!?, eyeing the e6-square.
12...♕f6 Offering a queen trade. With Black having less space, trading queens is probably a sensible idea, although at this point it is hard to tell. Either way, White refuses the offer politely.
13.♕d1
Also interesting was 13.♕h5!?, provoking ...g6 for abstract purposes.
13...♘f8 14.♗g2?!
Slightly odd, as later White moves the bishop to h3 anyway.
14...♘e6 15.0-0 White decides not to use the option of 15.f4!?, with very unclear consequences.
15...g5!

Now Black stops f4 and White starts feeling cramped, as he lacks pawn breaks and his bishops lack elbow-room.
16.♗h3
Finally White decides that tolerating the knight on e6 is not a good idea and sets up a trade on e6 before Black gets to shut off the bishop with ...h5 and ...g4.
16...h5 17.♗xe6 ♕xe6 18.b5

A double-edged move, pushing the knight back, but also losing more of the flexibility of the queenside pawn structure.
18...♘b8 19.f4

The opening of the g-file doesn't have any effect in the short term, since White's king can hide on h1, while Black's king can hide on the queenside. This, however, is just an expansion, trying to open some files for the major pieces and hoping perhaps that the b2-bishop will also see the light of day at some point.
19...gxf4 20.gxf4 ♘d7
Black finishes his development and doesn't have much reason to complain about the position.
21.♔h1 ♕g4 Black wants to establish some contact on the kingside, to castle queenside more safely, and not to have to worry about a4-a5 play.
22.♕f3

22...f6
Trading queens was safe enough, with Black having a very pleasant solid position, with a better pawn structure. But Carlsen is being ambitious here, and at this point rightly so.
23.♕e3 0-0-0

24.f5 An interesting decision. White gets tempted by the idea to send a rook to g6, but the bishop on b2 starts to look even more helpless now, with the position getting more closed.

24...h4 25.罝g1 豐h5 26.罝g6 罝dg8 27.罝ag1 罝xg6 28.fxg6

White initiates further changes in the position. Now he is hoping to trade the g-pawn for the h-pawn, obtaining a passed pawn. The problem is that he should worry about the weak d3-pawn in the process, with ...勾c5 coming at any moment.

28...罝g8

29.g7?

29.豐h3 was the right way to start. Now Black has a cunning option: 29...堂b8! (the knight is taboo due to the ...豐f3+ 罝g2 h3! motif) 30.豐g4 豐xg4 31.罝xg4 勾c5!, going for the d3-pawn. White seems to be ending up a pawn down here, but has good drawing chances once he gets some harmony, with 堂g2-f3, and then the h-pawn running down the board.

29...豐h7? Missing a huge chance. The g-pawn would not run away, while getting ...勾c5 in was essential. Very strong was 29...堂b8!. With ...勾c5 coming, it is hard to see how

A key game. When Magnus Carlsen's overly-ambitious attempts backfired, Nodirbek Abdusattorov showed no interest in a draw and successfully pushed for a win

White can avoid a collapse of his position. A sample line is 30.奧c1 勾c5 31.豐h3 豐h7, with g7 falling, followed by the d3-pawn.

Alternatively, 29...勾c5! also has the desired effect, since the tactic we have already seen will work here, too: 30.d4 勾e6 31.豐h3 堂b8!.

30.豐h3!

Now White manages to simplify into a very reasonable endgame, as he has the passed h-pawn to compensate for the weak d3-pawn.

30...罝xg7 31.罝xg7 豐xg7 32.豐xh4 勾c5 33.奧c1 c6 34.bxc6 bxc6 35.豐h3+ 堂b7 36.豐f3 豐h7 37.奧d2 堂a6

Black is hesitating a bit, waiting for the right moment to initiate simpli-

fications with ...b5 or ...d5. The position is roughly balanced.

38.堂g2 豐g7+ 39.堂f1 豐h7 40.h3 White chooses not to repeat moves. It is not clear if this was a winning attempt, as Black could also still deviate.

40...d5

A lot of simplifications are being initiated. A draw is now the most likely outcome.

41.♕f5 ♕g8 42.cxd5 cxd5 43.exd5 ♕xd5 44.♔e2

White is yet to send his h-pawn up the board, and in the meantime he has to take care of the d3-pawn. I would imagine that a ...♕g2+/...♕d5 repetition was likely.

44...♔b5 Maybe Carlsen wasn't sure he wanted the draw after 44...♕g2+ 45.♔d1 ♕d5 at this point, or maybe he got confused by 46.h4!? here. Either way, he chose to play differently.

45.♗e3 ♕g2+ 46.♗f2 ♔a4

Black is still well within the drawing margins, but he starts drifting a little bit.

47.h4 e4 48.dxe4 ♘xe4 49.♕f3 ♕g6 50.h5

The h-pawn starts to advance.

50...♕e8! 51.♗e3?!

This is either a mini-blunder or a draw offer – or perhaps both, since White was running short of time and a draw would not be the worst of results in this game.

51.h6! was a better try: 51...♘g5+ 52.♕e3 ♕h5+ 53.♔d3, and now Black

should not take on h6 because it is mate in 11, apparently, but instead keep the queen closer to the king. Amongst other moves, 53...♕d1+ will still hold here, although it is Black who has to be very careful now.

51...f5? A case of tactical blindness or a crazy winning attempt in the mutual time-scramble. 51...♕xh5! was an

A case of tactical blindness or a crazy winning attempt in the mutual time-scramble?

elementary draw. This is definitely the turning point of this game.

52.h6 Now Black has a very hard task ahead, since he has to try and juggle dealing with the h-pawn and looking after the exposed king on a4.

52...♕e5 53.♔f1 ♕d5 54.♔g2 ♕g8+ 55.♔h3

55...♘g5+ Maybe not a very practical decision. In the ensuing clear-

cut position, the youngster can now calmly play for a win, knowing he will never blunder a knight fork. Also, Black may well have missed the 61.♕g7! idea, thinking the text-move forced a draw.

55...♕g6 and keeping the status quo was maybe a more practical defensive attempt, but that was hard to decide during the game.

56.♗xg5 ♕xg5 57.♕c6+ ♔xa3 58.♕c3+ ♔a4 59.♕c4+ ♔a5 60.♕c3+ ♔a4 61.♕g7!

White is playing for a win. It is well-known that in queen endings, it is not the number of pawns, but about how far your furthest pawn has advanced, that determines who can play for a win. Here it is White, whose h-pawn is much further advanced than Black's pawns.

61...♕e3+ 62.♔h4

62...f4?

The computer prefers the immediate 62...b5, not allowing the powerful idea that White executed in the game. After 62...b5 63.h7 ♕e4+ there is a vague kind of perpetual: 64.♔h5 ♕h1+ 65.♔g6 ♕g2+ 66.♔f6 ♕c6+.

Undoubtedly still shaking from the drama they have just gone through, Magnus Carlsen and Nodirbek Abdusattorov mechanically begin to set up the pieces.

63.♕d7+! The move that won White the game. The direct pawn push 63.h7 was tempting, but after 63...♕e1+ Black does have a perpetual. Not at once, but apparently the white king cannot quite escape the checks.

63...b5 64.h7 Now the queen is not on g7 and the white king doesn't have to move in circles to protect it, and there is no perpetual for Black. It becomes impossible to force a draw, and just hanging in is a rather ungrateful task at this point, with only seconds on the clock.

64...♕e5? A losing move.

65.♔g4? This is good enough to avoid the draw and keep the pressure on, but there was a very sophisticated win available at this point: 65.♕d1+!!. First forcing the king to a3/b4 and only then going ♕d8 would apparently have won: 65...♔a3 66.♕d8 ♕e1+ 67.♔h5 ♕e2+ 68.♔g6 ♕e6+ 69.♕f6 ♕e4+ (69...♕g4+ 70.♔f7 ♕d7+ 71.♕e7+! is the reason we needed the king on a3/b4) 70.♔g7 ♕b7+ 71.♔g8 ♕d5+ 72.♔f8 ♕a8+ 73.♔f7 ♕d5+ 74.♔e8 ♕a8+ 75.♕d8, and now 75...♕e4+ is met by 76.♕e7+!, countercheck, while 75...♕c6+ 76.♔f7 ♕c4+ 77.♔g7 wins for White as well.

65...f3 Carlsen gives up the f-pawn to ensure there will be more checks against the king. 65...♕a3! was another defence, according to the engine, but at this point, in fierce time-trouble, it was impossible to understand what was going on.

66.♔xf3

The white king will eventually hide from the checks, although that doesn't necessarily mean it's a win for him, since he also has to queen the h-pawn. **66...♕f6+ 67.♔e4 ♕h4+ 68.♔d5 ♕h5+ 69.♔c6 ♕g6+ 70.♔c7 ♕g3+ 71.♔b7 ♕f3+ 72.♔a6 ♕f6+ 73.♔a7 ♕f2+ 74.♔b7 ♕f3+ 75.♕c6 ♕f7+ 76.♕c7 ♕f3+ 77.♔a6 ♕a8+ 78.♔b6** Finally the king hides from the checks, but Black keeps on defending.

78...♕h8! White's next task is queening the soldier on h7. **79.♕c2+ ♔a3 80.♕d3+ ♔a2 81.♔c5** Nodirbek is being very tricky, not grabbing the pawn just yet. Now Black should try to give a perpetual, or at least try not to lose by force. With the pressure and the clock ticking, Carlsen finally collapses.

81...b4? There is no point in doing this. Black had to start checking. The position would objectively still be a draw, even though it's a very hard job to defend this in reality.

82.♕d2+ ♔a1?? Although the computer points out that White is already winning, I don't believe the win would have been that obvious if Black hadn't blundered a queen trade. This move loses the game.

83.♕d4+! 1-0. What a fight!

■ ■ ■

Unreliable ratings

For various reasons, the rapid ratings are not always trustworthy, and they are certainly less reliable than the

Young Indian stars Gukesh D and Guha Mitrabha were more than somewhat underrated!

classical ones. This sometimes leads to weird situations. Young Indian stars Gukesh D and Guha Mitrabha have rapid ratings of 2050 and 2107 respectively. It is safe to say that, given the fact that they ended the tournament in 9th and 15th place respectively, they are – more than somewhat! – underrated.

The same goes for last year's Wijk aan Zee winner Jorden van Foreest.

Because of his lowly rating, the Dutchman had the toughest pairings of the entire tournament. Nevertheless, he finished in 12th place. Here is his fine victory over Alexei Shirov, with his own notes.

NOTES BY
Jorden van Foreest

Jorden van Foreest
Alexei Shirov
Warsaw World Rapid 2021 (6)
Ruy Lopez, Arkhangelsk Variation

1.e4 e5 2.♘f3 ♘c6 3.♗b5 a6 4.♗a4 ♘f6 5.0-0 b5 6.♗b3 ♗c5

Alexei Shirov seems to be playing the Arkhangelsk almost exclusively these days. As this was the first round of the day, I had been able to prepare for it a bit [as the pairings had been published the night before – ed.].
7.a4 ♖b8 8.c3 d6 9.d4 ♗b6 10.h3 0-0 11.♘a3

An unconventional move order, which I hoped would catch my opponent off-guard. Usually, when

White plays ♘a3 in this line, he does so on the previous move, so as to immediately capture on b5. However, as practice has shown over the years, Black gets strong counterplay in the form of a quick ...♗g4.
11...♗b7
Black had several other viable options. Considering them, Shirov used up almost four minutes, which is quite a lot for a rapid game. This rendered my little opening experiment a modest success already.
12.axb5 axb5 13.♘xb5
It was possible to strengthen the centre with 12.♖e1 instead, but I decided to go for more direct play.

13...exd4?!
This seems to be an inaccuracy. Releasing the tension in the centre is in White's favour, as the knight now gets access to c3. Instead, the immediate 13...♘xe4 was to be preferred.
14.cxd4 ♘xe4 15.♖e1 d5
This one surprised me, as now the bishop on b7 is permanently locked up. Keeping the bishop alive with 15...♘e7, and intending ...♘f5 seems logical and good to me.
16.♘c3
Black's central knight is his best piece, so exchanging it off is desirable.
16...♘e7 17.♗g5!
After considering rudimentary moves such as 17.♗f4 for a while, I suddenly came across this move that I was very satisfied with. Not only does it challenge the knight once more, but it also creates potential ideas of swinging the queen over for the attack with ♕h5.

17...♘xg5?! Quickly capturing the knight, but guaranteeing White a pleasant position without much risk. 17...♘f5 seems to maintain the balance, but it is not easy to assess that after 18.♘cxe4 dxe4 19.♕h5 ♘h6! Black is fully OK! For example: 20.♘xe4 ♗xd4 21.♗xh6 ♗xe4 22.♖xe4 ♖xb3 23.♖d1 ♕f6!, and the wholesale exchanges lead to a draw.
18.♗xg5 f6 19.♗f4

Despite having the strongest pairings of the entire tournament, Jorden van Foreest finished in 12th place, picking up 80 rapid rating points in the process.

19...♘f5?! Another mistake, leaving the knight hanging in thin air, as the threat to d4 is an illusion. Instead, it was necessary to drive away the strong bishop from f4: 19...♘g6 20.♗h2 f5!, intending to lock in the bishop with ...f4 and giving Black decent counter-chances.
20.♘a4!

Shirov had possibly underestimated this move. Suddenly it transpires that Black cannot take on d4 for tactical reasons. On top of that, he is about to lose his valuable bishop, after which his position will be left full of weaknesses.
20...♖a8
Perhaps it would have been better to attempt to save the bishop with 20...♗a5, although it would still not escape its dreaded fate after 21.♗d2!.
I was briefly worried about 20...♗xd4, as I saw a resource for Black, but White keeps a crushing attack: 21.♗c2 ♗e5 (the strong-looking resource) 22.♗xf5 ♗xf4, but White has 23.♕h5! g6 24.♗xg6 hxg6 25.♕xg6+ ♔h8 26.♘c5

ANALYSIS DIAGRAM

and despite being up a piece, Black is dead-lost, since he cannot avoid a crushing rook lift like ♖a4 coming next.
21.♖c1
Taking on b6 immediately was also simple and good.
21...♖f7
Once again, 21...♗a5 would have offered somewhat better chances of continuing the fight.
22.♘xb6 cxb6 23.♖e6!

The rook infiltrates, highlighting the dire consequences of Black's ...f6 back on move 18.
23...♖c8 24.♗c2
Forcing the knight away from its

outpost towards an awkward square.

24...♘h4

At this point, it was pretty clear that with my dominant pieces I should be able to win in several ways, but in a rush I thought I saw an immediate win.

25.♖d6?!

25...♖d7 I had completely missed this response, thinking that I would win the b6-pawn right away. Fortunately, the position retains all its pluses, and not much is spoiled after simply withdrawing the rook.

26.♖e6

Of course it would be a mistake to exchange the active rook for Black's passive counterpart.

26...♘g6 27.♗g3 ♖e7 28.♗f5 ♖xc1 29.♕xc1 ♕c8?

A final mistake, but the position was already objectively beyond saving. The white bishop pair is just too strong.

30.♕e3!

Now Black cannot avoid material losses.

30...♕e8

Here my opponent's flag fell, but 31.♗xg6 would also just win a piece.

The utmost praise

Back to where we left off! After Abdusattorov's sensational win over Magnus Carlsen, the lead was shared between Abdusattorov and Ian Nepomniachtchi with three more rounds to go. Ian deserves the utmost praise for his play in Warsaw. Coming from what must have been a terribly disappointing experience, he played as if nothing had happened. Perhaps his smoothest game was against Duda, in which he got to use some of his World Championship prep.

NOTES BY
Anish Giri

**Ian Nepomniachtchi
Jan-Krzysztof Duda**
Warsaw World Rapid 2021 (6)
Ruy Lopez, Marshall Variation

1.e4

Ian Nepomniachtchi had the luxury of being able to use his World Championship prep in the World Rapid & Blitz that followed so quickly after the match in Dubai. Jan-Krzysztof Duda decides to go for what had been Ian's stumbling block against Magnus Carlsen – the Marshall.

1...e5 2.♘f3 ♘c6 3.♗b5 a6 4.♗a4 ♘f6 5.0-0 ♗e7 6.♖e1 b5 7.♗b3 0-0 8.a4

Nepo may have run out of ideas against Carlsen here, but it is another story playing this in rapid against a player who didn't have a team of five

people working on this position for a week straight.

8...♖b8 9.axb5 axb5 10.d3 d6 11.h3 h6 12.♘c3 ♖e8 13.♘d5

So far we are still following one of the Nepo-Carlsen games. Curiously, White used the 10.d3 move order this time, instead of 10.h3, but that didn't really have any impact. Now, Duda does something strange – he chooses to deviate from the way Carlsen showed how to play this position in the match.

13...♘xd5 Not really an improvement. 13...♗f8 was what Carlsen played, and Ian probably had a better attempt ready for his next game than what he played in Game 7, which quickly finished in a draw.

14.♗xd5 ♗d7 Black loses a move, since he is unable to play ...♘e7 with the bishop on e7 disturbing the flow.

15.♗d2 ♗f6

Now Black uses this possibility. On f6, the bishop might be a tad more active than on f8, but it can also become a target of ♘h2-g4.

16.♖a6 ♘e7 17.♗b3 ♖a8

It makes sense to trade the rook, but 17...♕c8!? was an interesting alternative.

18.♖xa8 ♕xa8 19.♘h2

This move is an obsession of Potkin students. Carlsen had to face this manoeuvre against both Karjakin and Nepo in his world title matches. That said, perhaps I am reading too much into it, and this is just one of the main ideas in the Spanish, with Vladimir Potkin not to blame here.

19...♘g6 20.♕h5

Nepomniachtchi played all his moves pretty quickly, leading some to believe that he had been prepared all the way until the end of the game. That is unlikely to be the case, seeing that the computer clearly prefers 20.♘g4! here. The move Ian made, although very tempting, is much less accurate, according to the engines.

20...♗e6 21.♘g4

21...♕d8

Trying to keep his pieces closer to the kingside and intending ...♗g5, which is a human idea. But with the a-file under White's control it is not a very good one.

21...♗d8, not fearing the sac on h6, was stronger.

22.♗xe6 ♖xe6 23.♖a1

Ian Nepomniachtchi was impressive. Coming from what must have been a terribly disappointing experience, he played as if nothing had happened and tied for first.

23...♗g5?

This is awful, actually. The rook will be raging on the a-file. Black needed to go for counterplay with 23...d5!, when he would actually have a very fine position. The key is not to panic and not to fear the ♗xh6 sacrifice.

24.♗xg5 hxg5

In an endgame after the queen swap, the black queenside pawns would start falling. But now Black is also in a tight spot.

25.g3

Black has weaknesses and passive pieces and is just waiting for something to fall.

25...♘f8 26.♘e3

One step back, rerouting the knight. At this point, White already has multiple ways of gaining a winning

advantage, although I must say that the final combination in this game is a very pretty one.

26...c6

It is too late for Black to try and keep his position together, as there are too many weaknesses. Interestingly, the weaknesses are fairly circumstantial and only there because of the differences in the power of the pieces – mainly the rooks. Imagine the black rook having control of the a-file; then things would be completely fine for him.

27.♖a6 g6 28.♕f3 ♕c7 29.♘g4 ♕b7

Black should have at least gone 29...♔g7, although after 30.♕e3! things will still fall apart.

30.♖b6! A beautiful finishing combination. **30...♕a8** The point of the offered rook was 30...♕xb6 31.♘h6+ ♔g7

ANALYSIS DIAGRAM

32.♕xf7+! ♔xh6 33.♕xf8+ ♔h7 34.♕f7+ ♔h6 35.♕xe6, with a completely hopeless endgame for Black.

31.♘h6+ ♔g7 32.♕xf7+ ♔xh6 33.♖b7

And Black has no sensible defence against the mating threats against his king. It's a massacre!

■ ■ ■

Fabiano Caruana joined the fight for the top spots only on the last day, when he scored 3 out of 4 in his final

games – winning both his games as Black. The one against Grischuk had a lot of content.

Alexander Grischuk
Fabiano Caruana
Warsaw World Rapid 2021 (12)

position after 17.f5

Grischuk never shies away from a fight, but this time the rare 1.c4 e5 2.♘f3 backfired on him. In the diagrammed position it is obvious that the battery on the h1-a8 diagonal is spelling trouble for White.

17...♗h4 18.♖f3 g5
Very tempting! Yet, the serene 18...♗f6 preparing ...g5 or the simple ...h4, while preserving the option of taking on d4 at some point, was much stronger. White is simply defenceless.

19.f6!
Obviously, 19.fxg6 ♖xg6 was out of the question, but the text-move does a great job of turning an outright bad position into a bad but messy one.
19...g4 20.♘f5
The only move to stay in the game. The check on e7 and the fact that the rook on h6 is hanging are what White is basing his counterplay on.

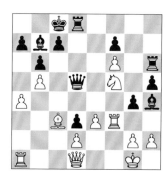

20...gxf3 Fabiano correctly decides to give up his queen for rook and knight. One can have a good time analysing this position! Interesting is the question of what happens after 20...♔b8 21.♘xh6,

ANALYSIS DIAGRAM

when 21...gxf3 22.♕xf3 ♕g5 23.♘xf7! ♕g8 24.♕h3 is winning for White. Black has better with 21...♕e4!!, with the idea of taking on f3 next, and, when the queen recaptures, to play...♕g6. White then no longer has the saving ♘xf7 desperado as in the line after 21...gxf3. Now 22.♘f5 ♖g8 (keeping the tension, 22...gxf3 23.♕xf3 would make things easy for White) 23.♘xh4 gxf3 (this looks very dangerous for the king on g1, but there is a way out) 24.♕e1 ♖g4 25.h3! ♖xh4 26.♕g3

ANALYSIS DIAGRAM

and with the rook trapped on h4, White is out of the woods.

The engine also points out the quiet move 20...♕e6, which goes to show the richness of the position.

21.♘e7+ ♔b8 22.♘xd5

22...f2+

This natural move turns out to be a mistake. I assume Fabiano was unsure what to make of 22...♗xd5 23.gxf3 ♖g6+ 24.♔h1, which does look messy with e3-e4 coming. Black, however, has a beautiful solution: 24...♖e8!!. This stops the push of the e-pawn (25.e4 ♖xe4!), after which it becomes obvious that White lacks moves. Black's next move is ...♗e1!, followed by ...♖eg8, with a mating attack. After 25.♕f1, stopping that from happening, the simple 25...♗xf6 suffices, intending to take on c3 and follow up with ...♖f6.

23.♔f1 ♗xd5

24.♗e5 A good practical decision, intending to secure the kingside.

24...♗xf6 25.♗f4 ♖g6 26.g3 ♗g5!?

This is not the moment to grab material with 26...♗xa1 27.♕xa1, when, with a4-a5 coming, the king on f1 is suddenly safer than its colleague on b8.

Fabiano Caruana won a game rich in content against Alexander Grischuk. The American was one of the four players who topped the table after the final round, but had insufficient Buchholz points for the playoff.

27.♗xg5

27.♗e5!? was perhaps preferable, and a draw offer of sorts, since it invites the repetition 27...♗f6 28.♗f4 ♗g5, etc. Black can play for a win with 27...f6, but then should reckon with 28.♗xc7+! ♔xc7 29.a5, which brings all three results back on the table.

27...♖xg5

28.♔xf2 Now Black will crash through, but the players were already severely low time at this point.

28.a5! h4 29.♕a4 would have kept the game going.

28...h4! Black is just much faster.

29.e4 29.g4 f5! doesn't help much.

29...♗xe4 30.♕e1 hxg3+ 31.hxg3 ♖f5+ 32.♔g1 ♗d5 33.g4 ♖g8

34.♕g3 ♖f3 35.♕g2 f5 36.g5 f4 White resigned.

Going into the final round, the standings were as follows:

		points	buchholz
1	**Abdusattorov**	9.0	87.5
2	**Nepomniachtchi**	9.0	85.0
3	**Carlsen**	9.0	84.0
4	**Caruana**	9.0	79.5

The tie-break rules

Considering the pairings, Caruana-Nepomniachtchi, Nakamura-Carlsen and Abdusattorov-Duda (with both Nakamura and Duda trailing by half a point), I expected fireworks!

Perhaps this is also a good moment to speak about the tie-break rules, which were to cause controversy. The regulations stated that in case more than two people tie for first, the two with the best tie-break (Buchholz – meaning the total amount of their opponents' points) play a match for gold and silver.

With this in mind, I was astonished to see a quick draw in the game between Caruana and Nepomniachtchi. While quite understandable for the latter – he was playing with the black pieces and had an excellent tie-break score – for Fabiano it essentially meant the end of any medal hopes and any title aspirations. It greatly puzzled me, but knowing Fabiano's fighting spirit, I am inclined to think that he was actually not aware of the tie-break rules that were in place.

Luckily, the other games did bring what we had hoped for. It turned out to be a tale of two rook endings! Carlsen, realizing the importance of the final round – especially given his worse tie-break – brought some deep prep to the table, immediately answering the question of what he had been planning to play in the World Championship match against 1.d4; the fabled Queen's Gambit! Still, the players ended up in a very drawish ending and there Carlsen got a sudden winning chance... that he didn't take full advantage of, letting Nakamura escape and reach a draw after 66 moves. A missed opportunity that will haunt the World Champion for some time!

In the meantime, Duda was making headway in the other rook ending against Abdusattorov. However, that game ended in a draw as well after Duda tried to cash in a bit too early.

Nodirbek Abdusattorov
Jan-Krzysztof Duda
Warsaw World Rapid 2021 (13)

position after 37.♖xg7

Here Duda played:
37...♖xh4
The final standings would have looked very different after 37...♔d4! first, optimizing the position of Black's king. Following 38.♖g4+ ♔d3, White is completely tied down. Now, for instance, 39.♖e4 ♖d6 40.♔g3 h5 41.♔f4 ♖d4, followed by ...♔xc4, will win the game. A big miss!
38.♖b7 ♔d4 39.♖xb6 ♔xc4 40.♔e3 ♖h1 41.f4 ♔c3 42.♔e2 c4 43.f5

And Abdusattorov had just enough counterplay to make a draw (½-½, 67).

Due to Duda's missed chance, an absolute sensation had unfolded, with 17-year-old Nodirbek Abdusattorov sharing first place with Ian Nepomniachtchi, Magnus Carlsen and Fabiano Caruana. As mentioned earlier, Caruana had a worse Buchholz, and so did Carlsen. And

so Nepomniachtchi joined Abdusattorov in the playoff blitz final.

This caused the World Champion to go into quite the rant on live Norwegian television, making it clear that he was unhappy with the regulations. The reader now probably expects a clear opinion from my side as well, but I'm on the fence. Yes, leaving Carlsen and Caruana out of the playoff did not feel entirely right, yet I have always found Buchholz a very reasonable way to determine the standings, as it says a lot about the opposition you faced in an event. To be frank, I did not feel that something majorly upsetting had happened.

But back to chess! The blitz playoff saw an absolutely relentless Abdusattorov. He drew the first game with the black pieces reasonably comfortably and, characteristically, struck in the second game when complications arose.

Nodirbek Abdusattorov
Ian Nepomniachtchi
Warsaw World Rapid 2021
(blitz tiebreak, Game 2)

position after 29...♖b5

30.♗e2! Redeploying the bishop on the a2-g8 diagonal, where it is much more effective.
30...♖b6 31.♗c4+ d5
A mistake, but 31...♔e8 32.dxe5 fxe5 33.♗e6! wouldn't be much fun either.
32.dxe5 fxe5 33.exd5 cxd5

34.e4!
Easy to miss in blitz and a typical case of pinning and winning! While the remainder of the game was by no means flawless – what do we expect from a blitz game with so much on the line – Nodirbek got the job done. Do try to spot the mates in two on moves 46 and 47!
34...♔f6 35.♗xd5 ♘xd5 36.exd5 ♔g5 37.♖e3 ♔xh5 38.♖xe5+ ♔g6 39.d6 a4 40.d7 ♔f7 41.♖f2+ ♔g6 42.♖e7 ♖d6 43.♖ff7 ♖d3+

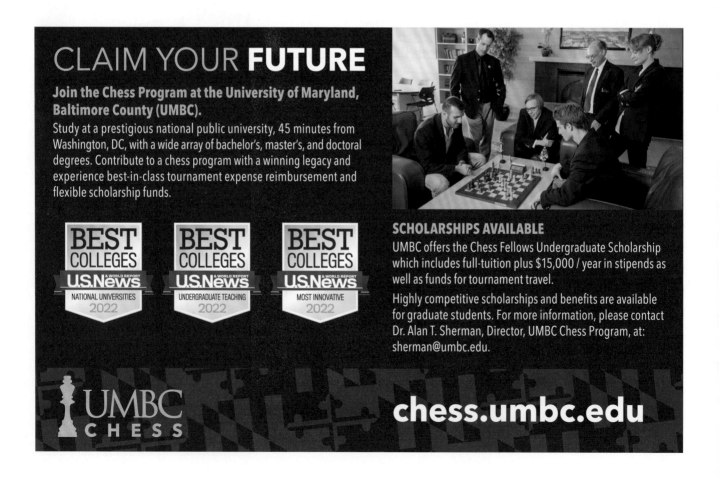

The sensation is complete. Ian Nepomniachtchi resigns the second game of the playoff and congratulates Rapid World Champion Nodirbek Abdusattorov.

RAFAL OLEKSIEWICZ

Warsaw FIDE World Rapid 2021

1	Nodirbek Abdusattorov	IGM UZB	2593	9½
2	Ian Nepomniachtchi	IGM CFR	2798	9½
3	Magnus Carlsen	IGM NOR	2842	9½
4	Fabiano Caruana	IGM USA	2770	9½
5	Jan-Krzysztof Duda	IGM POL	2801	9
6	Levon Aronian	IGM USA	2728	9
7	Hikaru Nakamura	IGM USA	2836	9
8	Shakhriyar Mamedyarov	IGM AZE	2727	9
9	Gukesh D	IGM IND	2050	9
10	Richard Rapport	IGM HUN	2750	9
11	Sergey Karjakin	IGM CFR	2757	9
12	Jorden van Foreest	IGM NED	2563	8½
13	Alexander Grischuk	IGM CFR	2763	8½
14	Vladimir Fedoseev	IGM CFR	2692	8½
15	Guha Mitrabha	IM IND	2107	8½
16	Daniil Dubov	IGM CFR	2735	8½
17	Maxime Vachier-Lagrave	IGM FRA	2773	8½
18	Saleh Salem	IGM UAE	2729	8½
19	Alexey Sarana	IGM CFR	2680	8½
20	Alireza Firouzja	IGM FRA	2656	8
21	Andrei Volokitin	IGM UKR	2631	8
22	Boris Gelfand	IGM ISR	2648	8
23	Ivan Cheparinov	IGM BUL	2621	8
24	Anton Korobov	IGM UKR	2689	8
25	Anish Giri	IGM NED	2767	8
26	Volodymyr Onyshchuk	IGM UKR	2687	8
27	Tigran Petrosian	IGM ARM	2621	8
28	Zahar Efimenko	IGM UKR	2609	8
29	Shant Sargsyan	IGM ARM	2344	8
30	Maxim Matlakov	IGM CFR	2652	8
31	Gabriel Sargissian	IGM ARM	2693	8
32	Kirill Shevchenko	IGM UKR	2508	8
33	Haik Martirosyan	IGM ARM	2377	8
34	Matthias Bluebaum	IGM GER	2575	8
35	Rasmus Svane	IGM GER	2677	8
36	Vladislav Artemiev	IGM CFR	2714	8
37	Maksim Chigaev	IGM CFR	2605	8
38	David Howell	IGM ENG	2624	8
39	David Anton	IGM ESP	2627	7½
40	Baadur Jobava	IGM GEO	2679	7½

176 players, 13 rounds

Abdusattorov wins blitz playoff 2½-1½

44.♔f4 ♖b8 45.♖xg7+ ♔h5

46.♔f5 ♖xb2 47.♖g8 ♖bd2 48.♖e1 ♖d5+ 49.♔f6 ♖d6+ 50.♔f5 ♖6d5+ 51.♔f4

51...♖5d4+

51...♖2d4+ 52.♔g3 ♖g5+! would have saved the game, but the clock was counting down fast at this point...
52.♔g3! ♖2d3+

53.♔h2!
Completing the mating net around Black's king.
53...♖d5 54.d8♕ ♖xd8 55.♖e5+ ♔h4 56.g3+
Black resigned.

And thus, the sensation was complete, Nodirbek Abdusattorov, the 17-year-old from Uzbekistan, was the 2021 Rapid World Champion. In his home country, this spectacular victory did not go unnoticed.

Upon returning home, Abdusattorov received a state reward consisting of a two-room apartment in Tashkent, as well as 250 million soums, which equals around 23,000 dollar. Much more importantly, this world title will be a gigantic boost to a highly promising chess career. Rustam Kasimdzhanov was right (of course!) with his assessment two years ago. This kid is the real deal. ■

MAGNUS CARLSEN TEACHES CHESS

Bringing the Banter

Banter Blitz, during which players comment verbally on their moves during a three- or five-minute game, is one of the greatest innovations to online chess. When two top players do battle, for example in the annual Chess24 Banter Blitz Cup, then just pull a chair up and be entertained watching the ups and downs from one of the players' perspective, with all the psychology in play – which can be pure chess gold.

There's yet another element to Banter Blitz that I really like, which is when a top player takes on all comers of varying playing strengths, and you get the chance to play a top player and listen to his or her helpful comments. It can be fun and entertaining, and someone might get a moment of glory by beating the pro. But above all else, it's a way for ordinary players to get a chance to play one-on-one with a top chess player, possibly even the World Champion himself!

Even I can have a fun night taking on all comers. My rule is that for lower-rated players it's a five-minute challenge, and with higher-rated players three minutes. And here's a top tip if you ever want to challenge me: If you have an entertaining playing-name, a curious one, or one that just makes me laugh, then you stand a good chance of me accepting your challenge!

My Banter Blitz opponent here is an FM [Emmanuel Neiman], who plays under the pseudonym of 'DocteurPipo', and he's from France. And with him being a higher-rated player, the game is three minutes, and that means there's less time for me to talk during it.

Magnus Carlsen
Emmanuel Neiman
Banter Blitz 2021 (16.3)
Petroff Defence, Nimzowitsch Variation

1.e4 e5 2.♘f3 ♘f6 3.♘xe5 d6 4.♘f3 ♘xe4 5.♘c3 ♘xc3 6.dxc3 ♗e7 7.♗e3 I'm going for the main line of the Petroff here – so let's see what he has in store, as I'm sure he's well-versed in opening theory.
7...0-0 8.♕d2 c6 9.0-0-0 ♖e8
A very reasonable move. Usually, White goes for a quick attack of some kind here, so let's get that running.
10.♗d3 ♘d7 11.h4 ♘e5
I think this is a very reasonable response. I could play 12.♘xe5 – but I want to attack!
12.♘g5

Now 12...♘xd3+ is logical, but I would go 13.♕xd3, with good prospects.
12...h6 13.f4!?
I just want to attack – I'm giving up this piece and hoping for some serious attacking chances. But I also had 13.♗h7+, which might have been interesting.

Even I can have a fun night taking on all-comers. My rule is that for lower-rated players it's a 5-minute challenge, and for higher-rated players 3 minutes

13...♘xd3+ I thought the logical move was 13...♘g4, and I'd go 14.♖de1 to keep the tension.

14.♕xd3 f5

Yes, I guess this is also a reasonable way to defend – but I'm just going to try to blow everything open now.

15.g4!?

DocteurPipo played 17...♕xa2 and MagzyBogues rounded off in style. Do you see how White pleased the spectators?

15...hxg5?! Best was probably 15...♗f8, but now he's taken the knight and that's opened the h-file – that has to be good for me!

16.hxg5 ♕a5 Now 17.♗d4 looks very good – it attacks g7 and generally opens the third rank for my queen to get over to the h-file. Then ♕h7+ will be a major threat. This will be very useful for me.

17.♗d4!

I might now have a threat of just playing 18.♖h8+!? ♔xh8 19.♕h3+ ♔g8, and 20.g6 may well be a decisive move. Basically, my conclusion is that my opponent is in a lot of trouble here!

17...♕xa2 Yes, what else did he have? If he had played 17...c5, that would have lost quickly to 18.♕c4+, and mate to follow shortly there with ♖h8.

Now, if I play 18.g6, there's 18...fxg4, when there's no longer any ♕h3 threats. And 17... ♕xa2 also helps with the defence, as he could have a resource in ...♔f8 and withdrawing ...♕g8 that might in some way hold. Let's just have a little think here, as I don't see it so clearly – I just don't see how he will defend if I go for ♖h8+!. Let's just go for that.

18.♖h8+! ♔xh8 19.♕h3+ ♔g8

His defence now is going to be based on some ...♗f6 idea.

20.g6

Yes, 20...♗f6 is hard to believe, as after 21.♗xf6 ♔f8! he has the annoying queen retreat back to g8 [Editorial note: in fact, just cutting off the retreat with 22.b3!! wins] that seems to hold... Wait, maybe I have

22.♗xg7+, but he could possibly just ignore it and run with 22...♔e7!? – it is all too late anyway, because he's played a different move, and we can deliver a nice mate now.

20...♗h4? 21.♕xh4

Now ♕h7+ is a massive threat. And if he attempts to run with 21...♔f8 this time, 22.♗xg7+! does work, since 22...♔xg7 23.♕h7+ ♔f8 24.g7+ ♔e7 25.g8♕+ wins.

21...♖e2

A nice attempt at counterplay, because he is threatening ...♕a1 mate – but now I get to deliver another back-rank checkmate!

22.♕d8+

I think that was pretty cool. Regardless of the evaluations, that was a good one. ∎

MVL keeps cool in World Blitz

In Warsaw, speed ace Maxime Vachier-Lagrave celebrated a career first as he won the World Blitz Championship. The Frenchman prevailed in the tie-break, dashing the hopes of local hero Jan-Krzysztof Duda. **MAXIM DLUGY** presents the highlights.

The final two days of the World Rapid & Blitz Championships in Poland's capital Warsaw were dedicated to the fastest of FIDE's world titles. A total of 21 rounds were played with a time-control of 3 minutes per game with two-seconds increments. At the end of this Blitz marathon the three Musketeers, Maxime Vachier-Lagrave, Jan-Krzysztof Duda and Alireza Firouzja tied for first place.

We will get to what happened then further on. First, I would like to mention the really sad story of the fourth Musketeer, Levon 'd'Artagnan' Aronian, who was leading the race for most of the rounds, only to stumble at the very last hurdle.

In Round 9 Aronian took the sole lead – and was to hold that position in Rounds 10 to 17 – by beating the eventual co-winner of the event, Jan-Krzysztof Duda. Levon did so in style, coming up with a flamboyant queen sacrifice for three minor pieces.

Jan-Krzysztof Duda
Levon Aronian
Warsaw World Blitz 2021 (9)
English Opening, Mikenas-Carls Variation

1.c4 ♘f6 2.♘c3 e6 3.e4 d5 4.cxd5 exd5 5.e5 d4 6.exf6 dxc3 7.♗b5+ ♘c6 8.♕e2+ ♗e6 9.dxc3 ♕xf6 10.♘f3 ♗d6 11.♗g5

A somewhat dubious novelty in this theoretical line, but absolutely typical of Duda, who prefers to keep the initiative. Instead, going for a slight positional advantage with both 11.♘g5 and 11.♘d4, followed by capturing on e6, was seen in a number of games.

11...♕g6 12.♗d3 ♕h5 13.h3
Here, 13.♗c4 and getting rid of the bishop on e6 seems more careful.
13...0-0 14.0-0-0? This was clearly White's idea, but now comes Aronian's cool refutation. **14...♘e5!**

15.♗e4 A nice finesse from Duda, but a little too late. The point was that after 15.g4, 15...♘xd3+ comes with check and Black will just be killing it in the endgame after 16.♕xd3 ♕g6 17.♕xg6 fxg6 18.♘d4 ♗xa2.
15...♘xf3 16.h4 The pin can be broken handily after 16.♗e3 ♕a5!, so White tries to keep the queen trapped.

16...♘xg5!! Awesome fireworks! Levon understands that the weakened position of White's king will make the standoff between three minors and the queen untenable for White. Now it's just a matter of technique.

17.♕xh5 ♘xe4 18.♕f3 f5 19.g4

19...♖ae8 The tactic 19...fxg4! would have won immediately, since White would be lost after 20.♕xe4 ♗f4+ 21.♖d2 ♗xd2+ 22.♔xd2 ♖ad8+ 23.♔c1 ♗d5.

20.g5 ♗c5 21.♖h2 ♗xa2 22.b4 ♗d6

The problem with fighting such a horde of pieces, is that any weakness in the position of the player with the queen becomes untenable if these minor pieces swarm to attack it.

For a long time Levon Aronian was the man to watch. The American was leading the race for most of the rounds, only to stumble at the very last hurdle.

23.♖xd6 cxd6 24.♔b2 ♗e6 25.♕f4 ♖c8 26.♖h3 ♖c4 27.♖e3 ♖d8 28.h5

28...♘xc3 29.♕f3 ♗d5 30.♕xf5 ♖f8 0-1.

Magnus Carlsen, possibly unsettled by the contentious end of the Rapid championship, was vulnerable in the Blitz and lost a total of 6 games

With so many rounds and with practically all the best blitz players present, drama and upsets were guaranteed. What to say, for instance, about Magnus Carlsen who, possibly unsettled by the contentious end of the Rapid championship, was vulnerable in the Blitz and lost a total of 6 games?

One of the turning points in the tournament was the brutal game between Aronian and Vachier-Lagrave. Levon completely outplayed his opponent and seemed to be on his way to continuing to lead the field after Round 17, but an incredible series of mistakes finally saw Maxime emerge victorious. Aronian not only lost the lead, he also got shaken emotionally, and the fight for first place began anew.

**Maxime Vachier-Lagrave
Levon Aronian**
Warsaw World Blitz 2021 (17)
Ruy Lopez, Neo-Arkhangelsk Variation

1.e4 e5 2.♘f3 ♘c6 3.♗b5 a6 4.♗a4 ♘f6 5.0-0 b5 6.♗b3 ♗c5 7.a4 ♖b8 8.c3 d6 9.d4 ♗b6 10.a5 ♗a7 11.♗e3 0-0 12.h3 ♖e8 13.dxe5

This quite complicated-looking line has already been seen in a number of GM games. As you can imagine, the engine evaluates all this as equal.

13...♗xe3 14.exf6 ♗f4! 15.♕d5

15...♘e5 Interesting, but our silicon friend prefers 15...♖e6!, with a couple of cool ideas.

To begin with, there is 16.♕xc6? ♗b7, trapping the queen.

And after 16.fxg7 Black has 16...♕e7! 17.g3 ♘e5! 18.♘xe5 dxe5!! 19.gxf4, and White is a piece and two pawns up, but the engine shows that after 19...♗b7 20.♕d3 ♖g6+ 21.♔h2 exf4 Black has enough compensation and initiative to hold.

16.♘xe5 ♗e6

17.♘xf7

A solid continuation, but another option was 17.♘c6 ♗xd5 18.♘xd8 ♗xb3 19.♘c6 ♖a8 20.♖e1 gxf6 21.g3 ♗h6, with roughly equal chances.

17...♕xf6 18.♖d1 ♕xf7 19.♗xe6 ♖xe6 20.♘d2 ♖be8 21.♖e1

21...h6

Levon could already have played the thematic 21...d5, with equality, but he prefers to make slight improvements to his position, since it's not so easy to see how White can save the e-pawn without giving Black excellent play.

22.♘f3 ♖xe4 23.♖xe4 ♖xe4 24.g3 ♗g5 25.♕d3 ♕c4 26.♕xc4+

26...bxc4 Black is clearly trying to play for a win here, as 26...♖xc4, followed by ...b4, would have been quite simple.

27.h4 ♗f6 28.♘d2

28...♖g4? In a blitz game, it's not easy to see that this is dangerous. The correct continuation was to give up the c-pawn and put the rook on b5, from where it would attack both the b2 and the a5 weaknesses. After 28...♖e5 29.♘xc4 ♖b5 30.♖a2 d5 31.♘e3 ♔f7 32.♔f1 d4 33.cxd4 ♗xd4 Black has no problems.

29.♔g2 d5 30.♖e1 Maxime had a great chance here to sideline the black rook for a while with 30.f4!, with the tactical idea of 30...♗xh4 31.♔h3 ♖xg3+ 32.♔xh4, which would have lead to a nearly decisive advantage.

30...♔f7

31.f3? White should have used the e5-square to improve his position and played 31.♘f3.

31...♖g6 32.h5 ♖g5

Suddenly, it's becoming apparent that Black is about to get into a winning endgame with 33...♖e5, so White decides to sacrifice a pawn to create counter-chances.

33.f4 ♖xh5 34.g4?! Quite dubious, since it would have been better to sit tight, but now Levon has to keep finding moves and losing valuable seconds on the clock while doing so.

34...♖h4 35.♔g3 h5 36.g5?!

Notice that at every instance Maxim chooses the objectively weaker move, which gives him tactical chances. If White captures on h5, Black would simply have a winning technical position in which he wouldn't need to spend much time considering options. But here, even if the position becomes completely winning, bad moves could get punished.

36...♖g4+ 37.♔f3 ♗e7 38.♖h1 ♗d6 39.♖xh5 ♖xf4+ 40.♔e3 ♖f5 41.♘f3 ♗c5+ 42.♔e2

42...♔g8?

Levon is seeing ghosts, trying to keep White from attacking the a6-pawn. This gives MVL chances of survival. After the immediate 42...♔g6 43.♖h8 ♖f8 44.♖h1 ♖b8 White would have had to start defending, which would have meant the end of any measurable counterplay.

43.♖h1 ♖f7 44.g6

MVL plays as actively as possible to create a potential mating net.

44...♖e7+ Levon correctly avoids 44...♖f6 45.♖h5! c6 46.♘e5!, with real chances of survival for White.

45.♔d2 ♖e6 46.♖h5 c6?!

This was the moment for simplification. After 46...♖xg6 47.♖xd5 ♖d6 48.♖xd6 cxd6 White will be lost.

47.♘e5 The surprising 47.♖e5 ♖xg6 48.♗g5 afforded more objective chances, as it's quite hard to break White's hold without allowing counterplay.

47...♗e7? Hard to say why Levon didn't attack the knight on e5. After the simple 47...♗d6 White cannot take on c6 due to ...♗f4+, so his position crumbles.

48.♖f5 ♗d8 After this, the initiative and the time advantage shifted to White.

49.♘d7 ♗e7

50.♘b8?! Once again, MVL decides to go for the most active continuation. Instead, the position after 50.♖e5 ♖xe5

51.♘xe5 c5 52.♘d7 ♗g5+ 53.♔c2 ♗d8 54.♘xc5 ♗xa5 55.♘e6 would have been a nice position to have under the circumstances, since Black is playing without his king, and one mistake could cost him the game.

50...♖xg6 51.♘xa6

51...♗d6? With no time left, Aronian takes his eyes off the ball. The a5-pawn is the enemy – play 51...♗d8! and win the game.

52.♘b4 ♗xb4 53.cxb4 ♖g1 54.♖f3!!

A super-tricky move from MVL, who is anticipating ...♖a1. Black had only one way to equality now, but a pre-move of the mind is sometimes as bad as one on an online site.

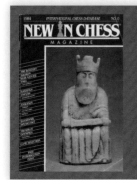

54...♖a1? Game over! The best way was 54...d4! 55.♖a3 ♖g2+ 56.♔e1 d3 57.a6 ♖e2+ 58.♔d1 ♖e8 59.a7 ♖a8 60.♖a6, and a draw is on the cards.

55.♖a3 ♖f1 56.a6 ♖f8 57.a7 ♖a8 58.♔c3 And Black's king won't make it in time. **58...♔f7 59.♔d4 g5 60.♔c5 g4 61.♔xc6 g3**

62.♖xg3 A slightly strange decision, but everything is working now.

62...♖xa7 63.♔xd5 ♖a2 64.♔xc4 ♖xb2 65.♖e3 ♖c2+ 66.♔b5 ♖c8 67.♔a6 1-0.

After this game Levon did not regain the lead until Round 20. When going into the last round he laid all the chips out on the table.

After a slow start Alireza Firouzja needed a five-game winning streak to get back in contention. Fiercely picking up speed, he finally ended up in shared first place with one round to go.

Going into the final round, the stage was set for one of the most intriguing finishes of the World Blitz Championship ever. Six players were tied for first place, all on 14/20 points: Aronian, Dubov and Artemiev, who had the

I cannot imagine a better feeling than beating the World Champion in a crazy game in the final round

best three tie-breaks, plus Duda, MVL and Firouzja.

While Duda and Firouzja were White against Artemiev and Aronian respectively, MVL faced the daunting task of playing the World Champion (albeit as White), while Dubov was paired with Anish Giri.

I cannot imagine a better feeling than beating the World Champion in a crazy game in the final round, clearing the road to eventually win the World Blitz Championship. And that's exactly what we saw in the following game.

Maxime Vachier-Lagrave
Magnus Carlsen
Warsaw World Blitz 2021 (21)
Ruy Lopez, Anti-Marshall

1.e4 e5 2.♘f3 ♘c6 3.♗b5 a6 4.♗a4 ♘f6 5.0-0 ♗e7 6.♖e1 b5 7.♗b3 0-0 8.a4 ♗b7 9.d3 d6 10.♘bd2 ♖e8 11.♘f1 h6

12.c3 MVL decides to go for this older continuation in this critical game, figuring that Magnus had loads of prep against Nepo's 12.♗d2, recently seen in their world title battle.

12...♗f8 13.♘e3

A less common move than ♘g3, but obviously very reasonable.

13...♘e7 14.h3 ♘g6 15.♘h2 d5

16.exd5 The first new move. The game Calvo-Pineda, Santiago 2002, continued with 16.♘hg4, the move fancied by Stockfish here.

16...♘xd5 17.♕f3

Maxime is continuing with his concept, used especially for this blitz tournament and seen in a number of his key games – he complicates the position to the max, even to the detriment of its objective assessment. In this must-win situation, I find this to be the best plan.

17...♘h4 18.♕e4 ♘xe3 19.♕xb7 ♘exg2 20.♖e4

What a feeling. In the final round Maxime Vachier-Lagrave defeated Magnus Carlsen in a crazy game and qualified for the playoff.

22.♕d5!!. An incredibly incisive move that simply threatens mate in two. Black must surrender material to stop mate. After 22...♖e6 (the only move) 23.♖g3! c6 24.♕xe6 ♕xe6 25.♗xe6 fxe6 26.♖xg2 ♘xg2 27.♔xg2 the position is resignable.
22...♕f5 23.♖xg2

23...♘xg2?

How could such an obvious move be a mistake? Well, Caissa created in-between moves to answer that question! If Magnus had 'lifted' 23...bxa4!!, he would have had a winning position in all variations. For example: 24.♗xa4 (24.♘g4 ♔h8 25.♗xa4 ♖ab8 26.♕xc7 ♘xg2 27.♗d7 ♕g6 28.♔xg2 f5, winning) 24...♖ab8 25.♕xa6 ♖e6 26.♕e2 ♘xg2 27.♔xg2 ♖g6+ 28.♔h1 e4 29.♗c2 ♕h3 30.♖xe4 ♗d6 31.f4 ♖e6 32.♖g2 ♕xg2+ 33.♗xg2 ♖e1+ 34.♘f1 ♗xf4 35.♗xf4 ♖xa1, winning.
24.♕xg2 ♖ad8 25.♘g4 ♔h8 26.axb5 axb5 27.♘e3 ♕h5

The position is actually slightly better for Black, but in a must-win situation this is a perfect scenario for Maxime.
28.♘f1 e4 29.♘g3 ♕g6 30.♗e3 ♗d6 31.♘e2 ♕h5 32.♘g3 ♗xg3

20...♕xd3

It would have been stronger to try to force a queen trade with 20...♖b8 21.♕d5 ♕xd5 22.♗xd5 ♖ed8 23.c4 c6! 24.♗xc6 ♖xd3 25.axb5 ♖d1+ 26.♘f1 ♘f4!, and Black is clearly better. This is quite a complicated line for even the World Champion to figure out.
21.♖g4

21...♕xh3?

This move allows an amazing winning idea for White, which was missed under pressure.
To keep a significant advantage, Magnus had to find 21...bxa4! 22.♗xa4 e4!, locking out the queen. Now White can still stay in the game if he spurns the exchange sacrifice with 23.♗xh6 e3! 24.♗xe3.
Now stop reading – set up the position and try to find the beautiful win for White here. It's really a move worth taking a break for.

22.♖g3?

After this White is losing once again. A better attempt would have been 22.♕e4, which leads to a roughly equal position, but the stunner I announced was:

33.fxg3 ♖d3 34.♕f2 f5 35.♗c2 ♖d6 36.♔g2 ♖ed8 37.♖h1 ♕g6 38.♗f4

Both players were incredibly low on time, but in the interest of objectivity, the plan of ♖h4-f4, followed by g4, would have given White excellent chances.

38...♖d5 39.♕e2?! White seems to have built a fortress on the queenside, but this move allows penetration. Correct was 39.♗b3, with a balanced game.

39...c5 It would have been far stronger to take the initiative with 39...b4! 40.cxb4 ♕c6!, threatening the beautiful ...♖d2, with devastation.

40.b3

40...c4 Once again, Magnus misses his chance. After 40...♕c6 41.♔h2 e3 42.♗xe3 ♖e5 43.♖e1 ♖de8 44.♕f2 ♕e6 Black would have won.

41.bxc4 bxc4 42.♖f1 ♕f6? 43.♕xc4 ♕b6 44.♗b3
MVL has finally equalized, and after 44.♕b4 he could have claimed that his position is no worse. The key, though, is to play active moves. Then, as we have seen many times, even the best players crumble under pressure.

44...♖c5? The winning move was 44...e3! 45.♕xd5 ♖xd5 46.♗xd5 ♕a5 47.♗f3 ♕xc3, and White will be unable to coordinate his defence against both ...e2 and ...g5.

45.♕f7! Suddenly White is much better and Black has only one move to continue the battle.

45...♖xc3? This wasn't it! The only defence was 45...♕f6 46.♖d1! ♖f8 47.♕xf6 ♖xf6 48.♖d8+ ♔h7 49.♗g8+ ♔g6 50.c4 ♖fc6, with reasonable chances of holding in a real-life tournament game.

46.♗e5 ♖d2+ 47.♔h1

With no defence against mates on g7 and g8, Magnus resigned, leaving Maxime in a tie for 1st-3rd place and a tie-break with Duda to win.

As Dubov made a quick draw with Giri, and Duda beat Artemiev, the following key game proved to be the end for Musketeer d'Aronian, who had been at the top of the standings from Round 10 and was tied for first before the last round. Alireza Firouzja once again showed the depth of his preparation, and when Levon faltered on the 15th move with the passive retreat of his queen, the current number two player in the world showed no mercy.

Alireza Firouzja
Levon Aronian
Warsaw World Blitz 2021 (21)
Italian Game, Giuoco Pianissimo

1.e4 e5 2.♘f3 ♘c6 3.♗c4 ♗c5 4.c3 ♘f6 5.d3 0-0 6.0-0 d5 7.exd5 ♘xd5 8.♖e1 ♗g4 9.a4 a5 10.h3 ♗h5 11.♘bd2 ♘b6 12.♗b3 ♕xd3 13.♘xe5

13...♕f5!
A strong move, showing that Levon Aronian had analysed both 13...♗xd1 and 13...♕g3, which had been played previously.

14.♘ef3 ♖ad8 15.♕e2

15...♕c8?

A serious mistake. Black should have made a tough decision between 15...♖de8 16.♕xe8 ♖xe8 17.♖xe8+ ♗f8 – with a very complicated but balanced position, which deserves further study – and the shrewd 15...♘d5! 16.♘e4 ♗xf3 17.♕xf3 ♕xf3 18.gxf3 ♗b6, with an interesting endgame, in which White's two bishops could have given him a slight pull.

16.♘e4 16.♕b5! was an even move powerful option.

After a slow start Alireza Firouzja fought back admirably to catch up with the leaders, but his tiebreak points were insufficient for the playoff.

16...♗e7?

Two retreating moves are too much even for the great Levon. He should have started putting up resistance with 16...♖de8! 17.♗f4 ♗g6 18.♕c2 ♘d7, when things are not great but not yet awful.

17.♗f4 ♖fe8 18.♕b5!

The queen finds this beautiful spot, from which it views both the kingside and the centre. Black is lost.

18...♗g6 19.♘eg5

White is threatening the obviously crushing ♘h4, when all bishops will be his and Black will be lost.

19...♗f6 20.♘h4! ♗xg5 21.♕xg5 ♗e4

22.♖ad1 It was also possible to end Black's suffering with the powerful 22.♖xe4 ♖xe4 23.♘f5 g6 24.♕f6 ♕xf5 25.♗xf7+ ♔f8 26.♗h6 mate.

22...♖xd1 23.♖xd1 ♘d7

24.♘f5 24.f3, winning material, was stronger. **24...♗xf5 25.♕xf5 ♘f6 26.♕b5 h6 27.♗c2 ♖e6?** The horrible position creates unforced

errors. Defending this position, in which White has two bishops for two knights along with dominating heavy pieces, is just too difficult.

28.♗f5

And Alireza won after:

28...♘e7 29.♗xe6 ♕xe6 30.♕xb7 c6 31.b4 ♘ed5 32.♕b8+ ♔h7 33.♕e5 ♕c8 34.bxa5 ♕a6 35.♗d2 ♕xa5 36.♕d4 c5 37.♕d3+ ♔g8 38.♕b5 ♕c7 39.♖e1 g5 40.a5 ♔g7 41.a6 c4 42.♕b7 ♕d6 43.a7 ♘c7 44.♗e3 ♘fd5 45.♗d4+ ♔g6 46.a8♕ ♘xa8 47.♕xa8 f6 48.♕e8+ 1-0.

And so, after 21 rounds, MVL, Duda and Firouzja topped the table with 15 points each, with the Frenchman

Warsaw FIDE World Blitz 2021

1	Maxime Vachier-Lagrave	IGM	FRA	2787	15
2	Jan-Krzysztof Duda	IGM	POL	2792	15
3	Alireza Firouzja	IGM	FRA	2810	15
4	Daniil Dubov	IGM	CFR	2749	14½
5	Levon Aronian	IGM	USA	2740	14
6	Shakhriyar Mamedyarov	IGM	AZE	2754	14
7	Vladislav Artemiev	IGM	CFR	2830	14
8	Javokhir Sindarov	IGM	UZB	2452	13½
9	Vladimir Fedoseev	IGM	CFR	2690	13½
10	Grigoriy Oparin	IGM	CFR	2580	13½
11	Haik Martirosyan	IGM	ARM	2707	13½
12	Magnus Carlsen	IGM	NOR	2892	13½
13	Martyn Kravtsiv	IGM	UKR	2638	13½
14	Alexander Grischuk	IGM	CFR	2757	13½
15	Mikhail Kobalia	IGM	CFR	2532	13½
16	Anish Giri	IGM	NED	2778	13½
17	Kirill Alekseenko	IGM	CFR	2663	13
18	Vidit Gujrathi	IGM	IND	2628	13
19	Sarin Nihal	IGM	IND	2705	13
20	Alexey Sarana	IGM	CFR	2672	13
21	Rauf Mamedov	IGM	AZE	2686	13
22	Aleksey Dreev	IGM	CFR	2641	13
23	Giga Quparadze	IGM	GEO	2658	13
24	Arjun Erigaisi	IGM	IND	2765	12½
25	Ian Nepomniachtchi	IGM	CFR	2792	12½
26	Mahammad Muradli	IM	AZE	2571	12½
27	Bassem Amin	IGM	EGY	2617	12½
28	Parham Maghsoodloo	IGM	IRI	2655	12½
29	Rasmus Svane	IGM	GER	2643	12½
30	Ahmed Adly	IGM	EGY	2656	12½
31	Ivan Cheparinov	IGM	BUL	2594	12½
32	Gukesh D	IGM	IND	2506	12½
33	Boris Gelfand	IGM	ISR	2647	12½
34	Alexander Donchenko	IGM	GER	2494	12½
35	Shant Sargsyan	IGM	ARM	2537	12½
36	Saleh Salem	IGM	UAE	2642	12½
37	Aleksandar Indjic	IGM	SRB	2603	12½
38	Hans Niemann	IGM	USA	2680	12½
39	Fabiano Caruana	IGM	USA	2803	12½
40	Vladislav Kovalev	IGM	FID	2527	12½
41	Maxim Matlakov	IGM	CFR	2614	12
42	Tigran Petrosian	IGM	ARM	2602	12
43	Volodymyr Onyshchuk	IGM	UKR	2657	12
44	Volodar Murzin	IM	CFR	2481	12
45	Jorden van Foreest	IGM	NED	2566	12
46	Nodirbek Abdusattorov	IGM	UZB	2686	12
47	Shamsiddin Vokhidov	IGM	UZB	2613	12
48	Sanan Sjugirov	IGM	CFR	2589	12
49	Vugar Asadli	IGM	AZE	2386	12
50	Dimitrios Mastrovasilis	IGM	GRE	2577	12

179 players, 21 rounds

MVL wins on tiebreak points

and the Polish favourite having better tiebreaks than the late-comer to the party, Alireza Firouzja. Much to the dismay of Firouzja's fans, the regulations stipulated that the winner of the championship was to be decided in a tie-breaker between Maxime Vachier-Lagrave and Jan-Krzysztof Duda.

After two hard-fought draws, MVL broke the deadlock with a nicely played game.

Maxime Vachier-Lagrave
Jan-Krzysztof Duda
Warsaw World Blitz 2021 (tb-3)
Ruy Lopez, Closed Variation

1.e4 e5 2.♘f3 ♘c6 3.♗b5 a6 4.♗a4 ♘f6 5.0-0 ♗e7 6.d3 b5 7.♗b3 d6 8.a3 0-0 9.♘c3 ♘b8 10.♗d2 ♘bd7 11.a4 b4 12.♘d5 a5

13.c3 Technically, a novelty. 13.♗e3 was played in Hovhannisyan-Halkias a couple of years back.
13...bxc3 14.♗xc3 ♘c5 15.♘xf6+ ♗xf6 16.♗d5 ♖a7?!
16...♗b7, swapping this strong bishop on d5, would have made more sense.

17.♕c2 After 17.d4 exd4 18.♘xd4 ♗d7 19.♘b5 Black would have

19...♗xc3 20.♘xa7 ♗xb2 21.♖b1 ♗xa4, with reasonable compensation for the exchange. White decides to prepare the pawn push to d4.
17...♗g4?
It was important positionally to thwart d4 with 17...♘e6!, with an equal game. In general, it's a good idea to stop your opponent's strategic plans in a blitz game, as it takes some time to come up with a new one.
18.d4 exd4 19.♘xd4

White should be happy with the opening now, as his minor pieces are clearly dominating. Black has an unpleasant defensive task in front of him.
19...♗d7 20.♘b5?!
A bit rash. White already has all he wants. He should have started preparing the central e5 advance with f4 or ♖fe1.

20...♗xb5? Probably the losing move of the Final of the World Blitz. Black should not have given away his position, while he could still dance around with 20...♖a6!, with only a slight edge for White, who had misplaced his knight.
21.axb5 ♗xc3 22.♕xc3

♔g7 38.♗c4 ♖xd7 39.♖xd7 ♔f6
40.b6 ♘e6 41.b7 g5 42.♗xe6
♔xe6 43.♖c7 Black has no chance,
since his rook is too passive.
43...h5 44.♔f3 f5 45.h4! ♔d6
46.♖h7 gxh4 47.gxh4 ♔e5
48.♔e3 ♖d8 49.♖xh5

Black resigned.

Congratulations to the New World
Blitz Champion, Maxime! Maybe it's
just me, but I think it's always great
when a Maxim(e) wins! ∎

LENNART OOTES

**Losing the playoff to Maxime Vachier-Lagrave was a bitter pill
to swallow for local favourite Jan-Krzysztof Duda.**

From this point on, MVL is unstop-
pable. His technique is quite amazing!
**22...a4 23.♕e3 ♕b8 24.♗c6
♕b6 25.♖ad1 ♖b8 26.e5 ♘e6
27.♕xb6 ♖xb6 28.exd6 cxd6
29.♖xd6**

Now, with a pawn to the good,
White simply needs to find another

weakness in Black's position, which
he does effortlessly!
**29...a3 30.bxa3 ♖xa3 31.g3 g6
32.♖d7** Hashtag xf7.

**32...♖b8 33.♖b1 ♖c3 34.♖a1
♘d8 35.♗d5 ♔f8 36.♖aa7**

Hashtag:-) **36...♖d3 37.♔g2**

COLOPHON

PUBLISHER: Remmelt Otten
EDITOR-IN-CHIEF:
Dirk Jan ten Geuzendam
HONORARY EDITOR: Jan Timman
CONTRIBUTING EDITOR: Anish Giri
EDITORS: Peter Boel, René Olthof
PRODUCTION: Joop de Groot
TRANSLATOR: Piet Verhagen
SALES AND ADVERTISING: Edwin van Haastert
PHOTOS AND ILLUSTRATIONS IN THIS ISSUE:
David Llada, Mark Livshitz, Rafal Oleksiewicz,
Lennart Ootes, Niki Riga, Eric Rosen, Anna
Shtourman, Berend Vonk, Michal Walusza
COVER PHOTO: Niki Riga
COVER DESIGN: Hélène Bergmans

© No part of this magazine may be reproduced,
stored in a retrieval system or transmitted in any
form or by any means, recording or otherwise,
without the prior permission of the publisher.

**NEW IN CHESS
P.O. BOX 1093
1810 KB ALKMAAR
THE NETHERLANDS**

PHONE: 00-31-(0)72-51 27 137
SUBSCRIPTIONS: nic@newinchess.com
EDITORS: editors@newinchess.com

WWW.NEWINCHESS.COM

MAXIMize your Tactics

with Maxim Notkin

Find the best move in the positions below

Solutions on page 84

1. Black to play

2. Black to play

3. White to play

4. White to play

5. Black to play

6. White to play

7. Black to play

8. Black to play

9. White to play

GIBRALTAR INTERNATIONAL CHESS FESTIVAL

Scheveningen Team Event **Battle of the Sexes**

£100,000 prize money!

WOMEN'S TEAM

Pia Cramling (captain)	SWE	GM	2457
Mariya Muzychuk	UKR	GM	2536
Zhansaya Abdumalik	KAZ	GM	2507
Antoaneta Stefanova	BUL	GM	2475
Gunay Mammadzada	AZE	IM	2459
Marie Sebag	FRA	GM	2447
Marsel Efroimski	ISR	IM	2419
Irine Kharisma Sukandar	INA	IM	2413
Olga Girya	RUS	GM	2402
Jovanka Houska	ENG	IM	2381
		Average	**2450**

MEN'S TEAM

Sabino Brunello (captain)	ITA	GM	2498
Bobby Cheng	AUS	GM	2550
Bilel Bellahcene	ALG	GM	2528
Leandro Krysa	ARG	GM	2523
Ravi Haria	ENG	IM	2497
Balazs Csonka	HUN	IM	2483
Joseph G. Gallagher	SUI	GM	2447
Gillan Bwalya	ZAM	IM	2404
Husain Aziz	QAT	IM	2357
Eric Rosen	USA	IM	2356
		Average	**2464**

Gibraltar International Chess Festival
For more information email chess@caletahotel.gi or visit www.gibchess.com
gibchess

Judit Polgar

Lessons in perseverance

Reaching a winning position is one thing, converting your advantage another. You need to continue posing your opponent problems and thwarting counterplay. **JUDIT POLGAR** shows how this is perfectly (and brilliantly) done in two prize-winning studies.

A well-played game typically features a confrontation of plans, sustained by hidden tactical resources. However, even in virtually perfect games, there is a certain number of 'impurities', e.g. 'superfluous' pawns or pieces, which at some point do not take part in the main action. These additional elements in a position sometimes make it difficult for the annotator or reader to spot and understand the deepest essence of the fight.

Things are 'purer' in endgame studies, where everything should matter and the economy of resources is essential. While solving or analysing a study is at least as hard as going through the same process in a high-level game, the study solver can identify the main elements of the position in their pure form. It is for that reason that solving studies develops your calculating and analytical skills, and is therefore a useful training method.

I will illustrate these aspects by examining two studies that won prizes at the recent Chess Artistry Competition that I organized in memory of Pal Benko during the 2021 edition of Judit Polgar's Global Chess Festival last October.

The first study is a good illustration of the relative character of the material balance. Strictly speaking, Black has a large material advantage, but in White's favour it can be said that pawns are known to increase their 'nominal strength' when getting close to their

> **Even in virtually perfect games, there are 'impurities', such as 'superfluous' pawns or pieces, which do not take part in the main action**

promoting square. Another important aspect is that the black queen is passive.

As the fight develops, we will see that White can only win if Black's hidden defensive resources are fully taken into account.

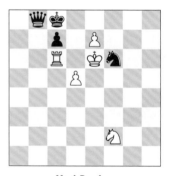

Yuri Bazlov
Chess Artistry Competition 2021
2nd prize
White to play and win

Since White is not facing the threat of an immediate check, he has the time to prepare his attack.

1.♘e4! The only way to maintain the rhythm of the initiative and get optimally coordinated. Apart from

The winners of the Chess Artistry competition were announced during Judit Polgar's Global Chess Festival last October. Part of the huge festival took place online, while hundreds of participants of all ages gathered in the Museum of Fine Arts in Budapest.

checks and White wins) 11.♔e7 ♕g7+! 12.♕f7 ♕e5+! 13.♔f8 ♕h8+ 14.♔g8 ♕f6+! 15.♔e8 ♕e5+! 16.♕e6 ♕h8+! 17.♔e7 ♕g7+ 18.♕f7 ♕e5+ 19.♔d7 ♕d6+! 20.♔e8 ♕e5+ 21.♕e6 ♕h8+, reaching a known position. The game is drawn.

The main idea of the winning move in the main line is keeping the rook on the sixth rank, thus preventing perpetual check.

4...cxd6 The part played by the rook is revealed in the following lines: 4...♕h8 5.e8♕ ♕h7+ 6.♔f8! ♕h8+ (alternatively, there is 6...♕f5+ 7.♕f7!. The queen swap leads to a known pawn ending and the last move also pins the enemy pawn, defending the rook. 7...♕c8+ 8.♔g7 ♕g4+ 9.♖g6. The rook finally arrives to help. 9...♕d4+ 10.♔g8, winning) 7.♔e7! ♕h4+ 8.♖f6. Once again, the rook is ready to protect the king. White wins.

Now, after 4...cxd6, things may seem to be simple for White already, but caution is still needed.

5.e8♖!! Forcing a transposition to a pawn ending, without offering Black any chance.

deflecting the enemy knight, this move also threatens an unexpected mate with ♘d6.

1.♔xf6? would run into 1...♔d7, clearing the eighth rank for the queen and reaching a draw.

1...♘e8 The most stubborn defence. 1...♘xe4 loses to the obvious 2.e8♕+ ♔b7 3.♕xb8+ ♔xb8 4.♔d7. Black will lose the pawn on c7, without being able to attack the d5-pawn, since his knight is dominated.

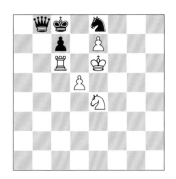

2.♘d6+! Forcing the black knight to get within the rook's range.

2.♔f7? offers Black a vital tempo for activating his queen: 2...♕b1! 3.♘d6+ ♘xd6+ 4.♖xd6. Here Black has several drawing moves. He can play 4...♕f5+ or 4...♕h7+, with a perpetual.

2...♘xd6 3.♖xd6 ♔b7! A cunning defence, setting some traps.

3...cxd6 loses to 4.e8♕+ ♔c7 5.♕xb8+ ♔xb8 6.♔xd6.

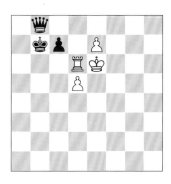

4.♔f7!!

In a practical game, it is easy to fall for the temptation to play 4.♖d8? ♕a7 5.e8♕. Amazingly, White cannot escape perpetual check here, despite being a rook up: 5...♕e3+! 6.♔d7 ♕h3+! 7.♕e6. The practical difficulty when evaluating this line derives from the fact that White has managed to activate his queen here. However, closer analysis shows that this is not enough to put an end to Black's checks: 7...♕h7+ 8.♕e7! ♕f5+! (8...♕h3+! may transpose) 9.♕e6 ♕h7+ 10.♔e8! (the best practical chance) 10...♕h8+! (the queen has to choose its squares with care. In the event of 10...♕h5+? 11.♔e7! ♕h7+ 12.♕f7! ♕h4+ 13.♔f6! ♕h7+ 14.♔f8, the white king escapes the

In the event of the obvious 5.e8♕?, Black defends with the brilliant 5...♕c7+! 6.♕e7 ♚a8! 7.♕xc7 stalemate.
5...♕c7+ 6.♖e7

6...♕xe7+ There is no stalemate after 6...♚a8? 7.♖xc7. **7.♚xe7 ♚c7 8.♚e6** And wins.

Perseverance and new threats

In order to win an over-the-board game after reaching an advantageous position, one usually has to display perseverance to maintain the tension and create new threats and problems against a stubbornly defending opponent.

This is the main issue in the second study, but we will also notice that White needs to be accurate when choosing between apparently equivalent continuations.

Evgeny Kopylov / Oleg Pervakov
Chess Artistry Competition 2021
3rd prize
White to play and win

White has a material advantage, and his a6-pawn is threatening to advance with decisive effect. On the other hand, the white king's exposed position yields Black reasonable chances of counterplay. The position looks natural and could well have arisen in a practical game.

1.g3! In the event of the hurried 1.a7? ♗b3+ 2.♚xc3 ♕e1+, the king cannot advance to d4 in view of ...♕e5 mate! And after 3.♚b2 ♕d2+ 4.♚a3 ♕xa5+ the game will be drawn.

The last move breaks the queen's communication with the e1-square and forces it to step onto an exposed square.

1...♗b3+! Before taking the pawn, it is useful to improve Black's coordination, while also confronting White with a crucial decision.

1...♕h7+ loses to 2.♕f5+, and White's pawn will queen soon.

2.♚c1! The only winning move, but also the most natural one.

It doesn't come as a big surprise that 2.♚xc3? leads to a perpetual check: 2...♕xg3+ 3.♚b4 ♕e1+ 4.♚b5 ♕e5+ 5.♚b6 ♕d4+ 6.♚c7 ♕c5+! 7.♚b8 ♕b4+ 8.♚c8 ♕c5+, with a draw.

2.♚b1? is insufficient for reasons explained below.

2...♕xg3 2...♕g5+ is parried with 3.♕f4, since after 3...♕xa5 4.♕f5+! the a6-pawn would queen.

Now, after 2...♕xg3, Black is active and even threatens mate in one. However, White has not exhausted his resources.

3.♕f6+! The start of an elegant series of checks 'around the knight'. The similar 3.♕e7+? allows Black to maintain the equilibrium on the edge of the precipice: 3...♔d5! 4.♕b7+ ♔e6! (in case of 4...♔e5? White has 5.♘xc4+!. The knight is taboo due to ♕b8+ or ♕c7+, winning the queen, and 5...♔d4 loses to 6.♕xb3) 5.♕c8+ ♔d5! (the careless 5...♔e5? allows White to return onto the right path with 6.♕h8+! ♔e6 7.♕f6+!, transposing to the main line) 6.♕c5+ ♔e6! 7.♕c8+ ♔d5 8.♕b7+ ♔e6 9.♕e7+ ♔d5, and White cannot gain anything concrete from the series of checks, and the game ends in what is called a 'positional draw'.

3...♔d5! The best practical chance. 3...♔xf6 allows White to win by simple means: 4.♘e4+ ♔e5 5.♘xg3 ♗a4 6.a7 ♗c6 7.h4, and the passed pawns on both wings yield White a technical win.
3...♔d7 also cuts the winning line shorter: 4.♕e7+! ♔c6 5.♕b7+ ♔xd6 6.♕b8+, with a decisive 'skewer'.

4.♕d4+! ♔c6!
4...♔e6 5.♕g4+ and 4...♔xd4 5.♘f5+ are simpler for White.

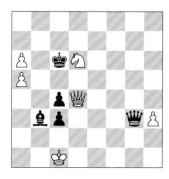

5.♕c5+! The only way of staying on the favourable trajectory.
5.♕b6+? is likely to transpose to the line after 3.♕e7?+: 5...♔d7! 6.♕b5+ ♔e6! 7.♕e8+ ♔d5, with a draw.

5...♔xc5
Black can no longer ignore the queen, since 5...♔d7 loses the queen to 6.♕c8+! ♔xd6 7.♕b8+.

6.♘e4+ ♔b5 7.♘xg3 ♔xa6

The play seems to have calmed down after the queen swap. Black 'only' needs to control h7 or h5 with the bishop in order to achieve a draw. Had White played 2.♔b1, he would have been unable to parry both ...♗a4-e8 and ...♗d1. With the king on c1, the latter is impossible and the knight can prevent the former manoeuvre.

8.♘e4!
8.h4? is ineffective due to 8...♗a4! 9.h5 ♗e8 10.h6 ♗g6, with a draw.

8...♗xa5
Sadly, 8...♗a4 runs into 9.♘c5+, exchanging the minor pieces and promoting the h-pawn.

9.h4!
Advancing the pawn is forced now. Continuing to play for domination would allow Black to save the game.

9.♘xc3? offers Black a vital tempo for approaching with the king: 9...♔b4! (threatening ...♔xc3, followed by ...♗c2, stopping the pawn) 10.♘b2 ♔c5, with a draw. This way of approaching the kingside with the king by creating queenside threats is reminiscent of a few famous pawn ending studies by Richard Réti.
9.♘c5? allows Black to free his bishop in time: 9...c2! (the only correct move order, since 9...♗a2? runs into 10.♘e4! c2 11.♘c3, gaining a decisive tempo and winning) 10.h4 (10.♘e4 is ineffective now due to 10...c3, clearing the bishop's path) 10...♗a2! 11.h5 c3 12.h6 ♗g8 13.♘e4 (threatening ♘f6) 13...♗h7!, with a draw.

9...♗a4

10.♘f6!
After this elegant move, the knight dominates the bishop, and the pawn queens.
10.♘d6? would grant the bishop too much freedom: 10...♗d7 11.h5 ♗e6 12.h6 ♗g8, and it's a draw.
1-0.

Conclusions
■ You should regularly solve studies in order to polish your calculating skills.
■ On the way to victory, you should permanently search for your opponent's defensive resources in order to sidestep them in time.
■ When having an advantage, you should keep pushing by continuing to create new threats and problems until you have achieved the desired result. ■

1. Xiong-Iturrizaga
Speed Chess 2021

26...♘f3+! An 'extended' discovered attack. White resigned. After 27.♘xf3 his rook is protected but his queen is not: 27...♖xe1+ 28.♘xe1 ♕xf8.

2. Shimanov-Aldokhin
Speed Chess 2021

31...♗d3+! 32.♔c1 ♖a1+! 33.♗xa1 ♕b1+! 34.♘xb1 ♖xb1 And Black checkmates being a queen, rook and knight down.

3. A. Mastrovasilis-M. Nikolov
Greece tt 2021

It's too crowded around the king: **28.♕xf7+!** Black resigned as after 28...♔xf7 29.♗d5+ ♔f8 30.♘hxg6+! hxg6 31.♘xg6 he is checkmated.

4. Chen Qi-Arjun
Asian University 2021

As so often, h7 is Black's Achilles' heel. White just needs his queen to join in: **21.♘f6+! gxf6 22.♖xe7! ♕xe7 23.♕g4+!** Ruling out both ...f6-f5 and ...♗e4. **23...♔h8 24.♕f5** Black resigned.

5. Csonka-Tologontegin
Speed Chess 2021

Black should act forcefully here: **33...♕d3+ 34.♖c2** Or 34.♔a1 ♖xa3+!, mating. **34...♕d1+ 35.♖c1 ♖xb2+! 36.♔xb2 ♕b3+** With 37...♕a2 mate to follow. White resigned.

6. Aldokhin-Ogloblin
Speed Chess 2021

20.♗xh7+! ♔xh7 21.♖h5+ ♔g8 22.♖xe5! Preventing a subsequent ...♘xg6. **22...dxe5** If 22...♘xg5 23.♖xg5 White is just a piece up. **23.g6 ♗f6 24.♕h7+ ♔f8 25.♖xf6+! gxf6 26.♗h6+** and mate.

7. Zlatin-F. Perez
Titled Tuesday 2021

21...♘e3! Obviously, the knight is untouchable, but the point is revealed after **22.♖xe7 ♕xf2+!** Or else Black loses! **23.♖xf2 ♖b1+ 24.♗f1 ♖xf1+ X-ray! 25.♖xf1 ♖xf1** Mate.

8. Galliamova-Bodnaruk
Russian Women's ch 2021

22...♗c3! 23.♖xc3 Now the queen is boxed in: **23...b6 24.cxb6 cxb6 25.♘xb6 ♕xc3 26.♕xc3 ♘xc3** Due to the hanging rook, White is unable to restore the balance. **27.♖xd8+ ♖xd8 28.♘c4 ♖d7** and Black converted the extra exchange.

9. Warmerdam-Yakubboev
Titled Tuesday 2021

The following line is strictly forced, but when going for it White had to spot a fascinating final position: **21.cxd5! ♘xf3+ 22.gxf3 ♕f4 23.dxe6+! ♕xd2 24.e7** With an in-between mate.

Thomas Willemze

Club players, test your decision-making skills!

What would you play?

When all is said and done, chess is all about the king. Therefore king safety is of vital importance. How should you act if your opponent's king is not in a safe place and you hope to exploit its weakness?

Opening up the centre is a very powerful technique to exploit a vulnerable uncastled king. However, if your own king is in the middle as well, you need to handle this technique with great care, since it might easily backfire.

Exercises

Uncastled kings played an important part in the game between Michelle Trunz and Eva Rudolph, participants in the Girls' Cup during the Dortmund Chess Days last summer. Both players left their kings in the middle until the very end, and it was up to White to assess whether she could open up the position to her benefit. I created four exercises in which you can experience how hard these decisions can be in a practical game.

Exercise 1

position after 12...g4

White has successfully bolstered the dark squares with her pawns and

is now ready for the next step. **How would you continue?** Increase the safety of your king with **13.0-0-0**, open the centre with **13.e4**, or keep the position closed with **13.c5** ?

Exercise 2

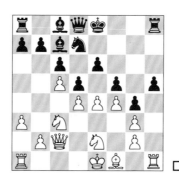

position after 15...f5

This is an instructive position that could have occurred in the game. **What would you play?** Grab a pawn with **16.exf5 exf5 17.♕xf5**, or close the centre with **16.e5** ?

Exercise 3

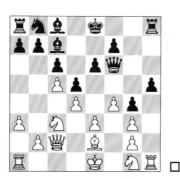

position after 14...♕f6

White has to make a choice regarding her king. **Should she play 15.0-0-0, 15.♔f2**, or leave the king in the middle and start pushing on the queenside with **15.b4** ?

Exercise 4

position after 17...a5

This sub-line to the game would have forced White to find the right pawn move. **Would you go for 18.cxb6, 18.bxa5**, or **18.b5** ?

I hope you enjoyed these exercises and feel more confident with uncastled kings now. You can find the full analysis of this game below.

Opening up the centre is a very powerful technique to exploit a vulnerable uncastled king

Michelle Trunz (1671)
Eva Rudolph (1818)
Dortmund Girls Cup 2021
Queen's Gambit Declined: Modern Variation

1.d4 d5 2.c4 e6 3.♘c3 ♘f6 4.♗g5 ♗b4 5.e3 h6 6.♗h4

6...g5

This aggressive move will soon give Black the advantage of the bishop pair, at the expense of a slightly weakened kingside structure.

7.♗g3 ♘e4 8.♕c2 h5

Black provokes a weakening pawn move before trading the knight for the bishop.

9.f3 ♘xg3 10.hxg3 c6 11.a3 ♗d6

12.f4

White skilfully absorbs the absence of her bishop by putting her pawns on the dark squares. An interesting alternative would be to ignore the attack on the g3-pawn and develop

a dangerous initiative with 12.0-0-0 ♗xg3 13.e4! ♗c7.

ANALYSIS DIAGRAM

This is an instructive position. It looks tempting to open up the position as quickly as possible with 14.exd5 cxd5 15.cxd5 exd5 16.♖e1+ to exploit the exposed position of the black king. However, Black can continue with 16...♔f8, quickly finishing her development with ...♘c6, ...♗e6 and ...♖c8.

Instead, White should close the centre with the counter-intuitive 14.e5!. This move slows down the development of the black queenside considerably and prepares moves like ♘h3 and f4 to open up the kingside, while keeping Black passive.

12...g4

13.c5

This move makes life a bit easier

for Black, since it removes the pressure from the d5-pawn and keeps the centre closed. The slow 13.0-0-0 would not have been frightening for Black either, because she can close the centre for good with 13...f5!.

The correct answer to **Exercise 1** was therefore 13.e4!. White will have a powerful initiative after 13...dxe4 14.♘xe4 ♗e7 15.0-0-0. Note that 13...♗e7 can be met by the aforementioned 14.e5!, followed by a quick f4-f5.

13...♗c7

14.♗e2

14.e4 was still the right move, intending to sacrifice a pawn with 14...dxe4 15.♘xe4 ♕xd4 16.♗c4, followed by ♘e2.

In case White protects the d-pawn first with 14.♘ge2, we will arrive at **Exercise 2** after 14...♘d7 15.e4 f5!.

ANALYSIS DIAGRAM

The conclusion of this instructive position is that White has no choice but to close the centre with 16.e5, with an approximately level game. Grabbing the pawn with 16.exf5 exf5 17.♕xf5 is extremely dangerous, because all the hidden energy

The aggressive 6...g5 will give Black the advantage of the bishop pair, at the expense of a slightly weakened kingside structure

in Black's position will be unleashed after 17...♞f8!.

ANALYSIS DIAGRAM

It is amazing to see how suddenly the black pieces restore their coordination and can expel the enemy queen, while finding their way to the most promising squares. After 18.♕d3 ♕f6 19.0-0-0 ♗f5 20.♕d2 ♞e6

ANALYSIS DIAGRAM

Black has a wonderful position and will follow up with ...0-0-0, ...♖de8 and ...h4.

ANALYSIS DIAGRAM

14...♕f6
Black protects her rook, but does not act against the upcoming e3-e4 break. The right move was 14...f5!, but I must admit that this was a dif-

ficult one to find, because it involves foreseeing the aggressive 15.♗xg4 and concluding that White is lacking pieces to join the queen in the attack after 15...fxg4 16.♕g6+ ♔f8 17.♖xh5 ♖xh5 18.♕xh5 ♕f6.

15.b4
This is not a bad move, but it unnecessarily deprives the white king of the option to safely castle queenside. The correct answer to **Exercise 3** was 15.0-0-0!, aiming to increase the pressure with e3-e4, before Black finds a way to coordinate her pieces. 15.♔f2 is a step in the wrong direction, since it allows Black to liberate her pieces with 15...e5! 16.dxe5 ♗xe5.
15...b6
The simple 15...♞d7 would have been the better choice.

16.a4
16.♞b5! would have been an elegant way to exploit the weaknesses in Black's camp. White will end up with an extra pawn after 16...cxb5 17.cxb6 ♗xb6 18.♕xc8+ ♕d8 19.♗xb5+.
16...♞d7
Black misses a golden opportunity to liberate her pieces on the queenside

with 16...bxc5 17.bxc5 ♗a5!.

ANALYSIS DIAGRAM

This is Black's dream. Her king is perfectly safe in the middle and her minor pieces can finally move to comfortable squares with, for instance, ...♞a6-b4 and ...♗a6.
17.♗d3 bxc5!
Well played! This move is far stronger than 17...a5, which would have led to **Exercise 4**.

ANALYSIS DIAGRAM

The correct answer was 18.b5!, to prepare opening the queenside without activating the black minor pieces.

ANALYSIS DIAGRAM

White is much better after 18...♗b7

19.bxc6 ♗xc6 20.cxb6 ♗xb6 21.♘e4!. Note that both 18.cxb6 ♗xb6 and 18.bxa5 bxc5! would liberate the black pieces and give Black a pleasant position.

18.bxc5

18...a5

This is bad news for the black dark-squared bishop. 18...♗a5! was required, to pin the white knight and complicate the e3-e4-pawn break. For instance, 19.♘ge2 ♖b8 20.e4 would allow Black to strike in the centre with 20...♘xc5! 21.dxc5 d4.

19.♖b1 ♖b8 20.♘ge2 ♖xb1+ 21.♕xb1

21...♘b8

It makes a lot of sense to direct the knight to the beautiful b4-square, but this plan is relatively slow and fails to address the central pawn break. It was therefore better to develop counterplay on the kingside with 21... h4 22.gxh4 ♖xh4 23.♔d2 ♕h8!.

22.♔d2

There was no need to postpone 22.e4! any longer. White has a promising position after 22...♕e7 23.e5!, hoping

to push f4-f5 in the next couple of moves.

22...♔d7

23.e4!

Simple and strong, and therefore much more practical than the entertaining 23.♘b5 cxb5 24.axb5.

23...dxe4 24.♘xe4 ♕e7 25.♖h4

25...f5

This move severely weakens the black position and makes her defence problematic. Trading the light-squared bishops with 25...♗a6 would have been a better try.

26.♘g5 ♘a6

27.♗xf5

Well played! From now on, White

does not grant her opponent a single chance of survival.

27...♖e8

Black could not accept the sacrifice on account of 27...exf5 28.♕xf5+ ♔d8 29.♘f7+ ♔e8 30.♕xc8+ ♔xf7 31.♕xh8.

28.♗xg4 ♕f6 29.♖xh5 ♖g8 30.♕e4 ♘b4 31.♗xe6 ♗xe6 32.♕xe6+ ♕xe6 33.♘xe6 ♘d5

34.♖xd5!

This small combination gives White two knights and five (!) pawns for the rook and decides the game.

34...cxd5 35.♘xc7+ ♔d7 36.♘xd5

Black resigned.

Conclusion

This game demonstrated how opening up the centre against an uncastled king is all about staying in control and making sure your opponent cannot develop counterplay. ■

Opening up the centre against an uncastled king is all about staying in control and making sure your opponent cannot develop counterplay

They are The Champions

GREECE
Population: 11 million
Rated players: 25,000

HARITOMENI MARKANTONAKI
Greece

The 2021 Greek Women's Champion is WFM Haritomeni Markantonaki. It was Haritomeni's third title after winning the championship in 2014 and 2019. In 2020, the tournament did not take place because of Covid. The championship was played in the first half of December in Lamia, a small city approximately 200 kilometres north of Athens. The tournament was a 10-player round-robin.

Haritomeni started strongly with a win over the highest-rated player Ekaterini Pavlidou, but then lost in the second round after a tactical oversight against Ioulia Makka. Her sixth-round game against Marina Makropoulou was crucial. Marina was leading the tournament, and Haritomeni beat her, showing excellent endgame technique.

Haritomeni Markantonaki (2133)
Marina Makropoulou (2182)
Lamia, Greek Women's
Championship 2021

position after 30...d4

White is a pawn up, but which pawns are more dangerous: White's queenside passers or Black's central pawns? White first blocks her opponent's pawns and then wins by advancing her queenside pawns.

31.♔g1! It is crucial to activate the king and stop the advance of Black's passed pawns in the centre. 31.b5 ♖d8 32.♔g1 d3 33.♖a1 e4 34.♔f2 f5 is less clear, as White's rook has to continue to support the king in stopping Black's pawns.
31...♖d8 32.♔f2 d3 33.♖a1 e4 34.f5! Preventing Black from securing her pawn chain with ...f5.
34...g6 35.g4 gxf5 36.gxf5 d2 37.♖d1 ♖d3 38.♔e2 ♖f3 39.♖xd2 ♖xf5 40.♔e3 ♖e5 41.c4 ♔f7 42.c5 f5 43.c6 ♖e8 44.b5 ♔e6 45.c7 ♔e5 46.♖d8 1-0.

In the end, Haritomeni won the championship convincingly, with a round to spare and 7 out of 9 points, a full point ahead of Ekaterini Pavlidou.

Haritomeni works as an electrical engineer for the Ministry of Finance.

After her work from seven a.m. to three p.m. she tries to study two to three hours of chess every day. Haritomeni represented Greece at four Chess Olympiads: Tromsø, Batumi, Baku and the online Olympiad in 2020. She still cherishes the memory of the Tromsø Chess Olympiad in 2014. It was her first time representing Greece at an Olympiad, and she enjoyed playing with all the different countries and top players in one hall. Furthermore, she started the tournament with a perfect 5 out of 5.

A friend of her parents invited Haritomeni to a chess club at the age of seven. She was a fast learner and quickly started to win tournaments and Greek youth championships. She has been passionate about chess ever since. Haritomeni likes chess because chess supports her memory, thinking and focus in everyday life. In addition, she likes to travel for chess and meet new people and is proud to represent her country. Besides a lover of chess, Haritomeni is a big soccer fan and attends matches of the national team and her favourite club, AEK. Next to soccer, she likes to read Greek fiction.

Despite her full-time job, Haritomeni still has ambitious chess goals. She aims for the women's grandmaster title, winning more national titles, and continuing to represent the Greek national team for many years to come. She is already looking forward to the 2022 Chess Olympiad this summer in Moscow, that will run from July 26 to August 7. ∎

In **They are The Champions** we pay tribute to national champions across the globe. For suggestions please write to editors@newinchess.com.

Horrifically fascinating

Amid the recent books that he reviews, the second volume of *Masterpieces and Dramas of the Soviet Championships* (1938-1947) stands out for **MATTHEW SADLER** 'This book gives an amazing insight into how Russian chess players and players from surrounding regions coped with the profound effects of the war – effects that obviously had a huge general impact, but also often reached deep into their personal lives and profession.'

The World Championship has ended but chess marches on! After a couple of days over Christmas watching the space-age Chess960 prowess of the TCEC engines, the World Rapid and Blitz championships in Warsaw were next up to assuage my chess hunger! The event itself was extremely dramatic, but something else that caught my eye was a tweet from Maxime Vachier-Lagrave criticising the inadequate arrangements for transferring the players back to the hotel after the games had finished. I'm certainly not underplaying MVL's complaints – as a professional, I also found wasting time for preparation by hanging around aimlessly to be extremely draining – but I allowed myself a wry smile, engrossed as I was in reading two books detailing a period in Russian (chess) history when – for some players – just playing chess, keeping the titles you had earned, staying out of prison or even staying alive was far from a certainty.

I'm talking about *Petr Izmailov: From Chess Champion of Russia to Enemy of the People. The Truth about my Father* by Nikolai Izmailov and *Masterpieces and Dramas of the Soviet Championships, Volume II (1938-1947)* by Sergey Voronkov, both books published by Elk and Ruby.

As a professional, I tried extremely hard at every tournament to create the best conditions for myself to perform optimally. I created a fixed and quiet routine everywhere I went, hoping to minimise distractions and create maximum focus on my chess. It was something that I drew strength from during the game: if I'd executed my routine properly, I felt somehow that I had the right to get what I wanted from the game. Likewise, I would easily get stressed if my routine was broken for some reason and this would often have a negative effect on my play.

Look through a book of the World Championships as a young kid, you see Alekhine losing to Euwe in 1935, you read (possibly scurrilous) stories of Alekhine being drunk during some games, and with the cruelty of youth you declare him a 'loser'. Look back on the match as a professional, and you can imagine yourself turning to drink only too well after having to play 30 games in 13 different cities in a foreign country in two months, never able to settle into a rhythm, never able to find harmony, while facing an opponent of unexpected World Championship calibre!

By the same token, you see the result of the 1941 Match Tournament for the title of Soviet Absolute Champion and it's totally clear how much better Botvinnik was than the other players (he won the tournament with 13½/20 ahead of Keres with 11/20 and Smyslov on 10/20). It's only when reading *Masterpieces and Dramas* that you learn how much

For some players – just playing chess, staying out of prison or even staying alive was far from a certainty

earlier Botvinnik knew about the tournament taking place than the other players (it was his idea!) and how much more intensively he'd been able to prepare! I think it's fair to say that all of the players who became World Champion possessed extraordinary qualities, but it's the joy of books like this that they help you understand the extraordinary qualities and difficult circumstances of the players who didn't quite make it.

We'll start with *Petr Izmailov: From Chess Champion of Russia to Enemy of the People. The Truth about my Father.* If you have never heard of Petr Izmailov, you're no different to 99% of chess players! Izmailov was one of Russia's strongest players in the late 1920s, winning the championship of Soviet Russia in 1928 and then qualifying for the finals of the 6th Russian Championship in 1929, beating an already strong 18-year-old Botvinnik along the way. It should have been the pinnacle of Izmailov's career thus far, but for murky reasons he never took part in the final. Some sources claimed he was exhausted or ill, others said he declined or 'couldn't' play.

Nikolai Izmailov recalls a conversation with his mother 50 years after the championship ended, in which she recalled Petr saying that he was healthy and eager to play but that he had been ordered to leave the tournament in a harsh, categorical tone that left no option but to comply. Nikolai Izmailov speculates that as the son of a clergyman, Petr could not be allowed to become the champion of the Soviet state of peasants and workers. Taking into account his ultimate tragic fate, it doesn't seem far-fetched. Izmailov was arrested in September 1936, accused of being a member of a 'counter-revolutionary Trotskyist-fascist terrorist organisation', and, after a brief trial, shot on 28th April 1937.

This book gathers together all of Izmailov's surviving games with

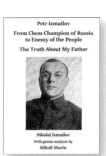

Petr Izmailov: From Chess Champion of Russia to Enemy of the People. The Truth about my Father
Nikolai Izmailov
Elk and Ruby, 2021
★★★★☆

annotations by the always excellent Mihail Marin as well as contemporary notes from players such as Yuri Averbakh. A paltry 25 games survive, of which 8 wins, 3 draws and 14 losses! Why the imbalance? Since Izmailov's own archive was lost (for obvious reasons) all these games were gleaned from other publications. Izmailov was by far the strongest player in the Siberian region, which made any wins against him more newsworthy and publishable than his wins! There's also a mass of biographical detail including many photos giving a wonderful insight into Russian chess life in the 1920s and 1930s seen through the eyes and career of a strong master.

In the 1931 Soviet Championship semi-finals, Izmailov failed to qualify, ending shared 3rd-5th, but he did have the satisfaction of extending his personal score against Botvinnik (who qualified for and then won his first Soviet Championship final) to 2-0! Botvinnik blamed this loss on the upset of losing to Konstantinopolsky the previous day, a defeat caused by 'eating too much'(!). It looks more to me as if Botvinnik was driven into panic by losing his way in a sharp and unusual middlegame.

Peter Nikolaevich Izmailov
Mikhail Botvinnik
Moscow Soviet Championship
semi-finals 1931
Queen's Indian Defence

1.d4 ♘f6 2.♘f3 b6 3.c4 ♗b7 4.♘c3 e6 5.♗g5 ♗e7
Botvinnik was somewhat unsettled against this line throughout his career, choosing 5...h6 6.♗h4 ♗b4

against Flohr in 1936 before losing to Uhlmann at Varna 1962 after 5...h6 6.♗h4 g5 7.♗g3 ♘h5.
6.♕c2 h6 7.♗xf6 ♗xf6 8.e4 d6 9.e5

A bold idea that runs the risk of over-reaching. It seems to unnerve Botvinnik, however, who soon make a serious mistake.
9...♗e7 10.♖d1 ♘d7 11.♗d3 ♕c8
11...dxe5 12.dxe5 ♗xf3 13.gxf3 ♘xe5 14.♗e4 ♗d6 is a possible exchange sacrifice pointed out by Marin with good compensation for Black.
12.♗e4 c6

13.♕e2
13.d5 was extremely powerful. Intuitively, you would expect that the opposition of the queens on the c-file would slow down White's play. However, the black queen's specific placement on c8 and the weakening of the kingside light squares caused by 6...h6 gives White a sneaky tactical opportunity! 13...cxd5 14.cxd5 exd5 15.♗f5 ♕c7 (15...dxe5 16.♘xe5 is the key point) 16.e6, with powerful play against Black's kingside and central light squares.

13...♕c7 14.0-0 dxe5 15.dxe5 0-0-0 16.♗c2 g5

After the initial scare, Botvinnik plays in resolute and concrete fashion, undermining White's support of the e5-pawn. Black's main dilemma in the position looking forwards is how to activate both his knight and his light-squared bishop. ...♘c5 blocks the a8-h1 diagonal and ...c5 takes away the knight's best square!

17.♖fe1 g4 18.♘d4 ♖hg8 19.f4

It feels risky to open the g-file, but White's boldness seems to confuse Botvinnik, who hesitates between kingside action and the desire to secure active squares for his queenside minor pieces.

19...gxf3 20.♘xf3

20...♗b4

20...♖g7 21.♖d2 ♖dg8 22.♕d3 f5 was my engine's simple way of getting things moving. If White captures on f6, the black knight gets active that way allowing ...c5 without any drawbacks! Botvinnik starts to mess around positionally, doubling White's c-pawns in order to secure the c5-square for his knight. However, Black lacks a follow-

up while White has a surprisingly annoying target in Black's isolated h-pawn!

21.♔h1 ♖g4 22.h3 ♖g3 23.♖d2 ♗xc3 24.bxc3 ♖dg8 25.♕e3 h5

25...c5 26.♗e4.

26.a4

It looks more natural to me to keep on going after the h-pawn, but Izmailov decides to play on both wings, softening up Black's king's position with a5, undermining the knight on the outpost that Botvinnik has proudly created!

26...♔b8 27.♖ed1 ♘c5 28.a5 ♕e7 29.axb6 axb6 30.♕f4

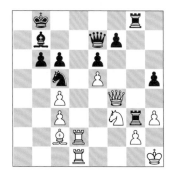

Black's knight is pinned to c5 now as d7 has to be defended. This means, however, that Black's light-squared bishop will never be active. Black's rooks are active on the g-file but their pressure against g2 – lacking the support of a diagonal piece – is easily countered. And White has a little shocker up his sleeve!

30...♔c7 31.♔h2 ♗a6 32.♗h7

A surprising shot! The idea is 32...♖8g7 33.♕f6, which looks completely killing! However, Marin takes Averbakh's annotations further

and finds a miraculous drawing line for Black: 33...♕xf6 34.exf6 ♖xh7 35.♔xg3 ♘e4+ 36.♔h4 ♘xd2 37.♖xd2 ♖h6 38.♘e5 ♖xf6 39.♖d7+ ♔b8 40.♖xf7 ♖xf7 41.♘xf7 ♗c4 42.♘e5 ♗f1 43.♔xh5 ♗xg2 44.h4 ♗f1 45.♔g5 ♗e2 and Black is just in time to halt the h-pawn and swap off White's last remaining pawn: 46.♘g4 b5 47.h5 c5 48.h6 ♗d3 49.♘e5 ♗h7 50.♘d7+ ♔c7 51.♘f8 b4 52.cxb4 cxb4 53.♘xh7 b3 54.♘f6 b2 55.h7 b1♕ 56.h8♕ and this is drawn of course! Botvinnik's reply is sheer panic and loses without a fight!

32...♖3g7 33.♗xg8 ♖xg8 34.♖d4 ♗c8 35.♕h6 ♘d7 36.♖f4 c5 37.♕xh5 ♖g7 38.♖g4 f5 39.♖xg7 ♕xg7 40.♖e1 ♗b7 41.♕g5 ♕h8 42.♕e7 ♕h6 43.♕d6+ ♔c8 44.♖d1 ♕f4+ 45.g3

1-0. A very convincing game!

A really lovely book, warmly recommended: 4 stars!

■ ■ ■

That was great, but *Masterpieces and Dramas of the Soviet Championships, Volume II (1938-1947)* by Sergey Voronkov is even better. I'll say it already – it's a real 5 star book!

The period before and during the Second World War is obviously both a horrific and horrifically fascinating period of European history. This book gives an amazing insight into how Russian chess players and players from surrounding regions coped with the profound effects of the war – effects that obviously had a huge general impact, but also often reached deep into their personal lives and professions. Take the Estonian Paul Keres, before the start of the war generally seen as the most likely next challenger for Alekhine together with Botvinnik. His country was occupied by the Russians in 1940 and he was 'welcomed' into the 12th Soviet Championship of 1940 (along with Petrovs from Latvia and Mikenas from Lithuania) where he finished 4th. Estonia was 'liberated' by Nazi

Masterpieces and
Dramas of the Soviet
Championships
Volume II (1938-1947)
Sergey Voronkov
Elk and Ruby, 2021
★★★★★

Germany in 1941 and Keres played in five tournaments in Germany in the next few years. He was playing in (neutral) Sweden in 1944 but returned to Tallinn in July 1944 to be with his wife and daughter when Soviet forces reoccupied Estonia in September 1944. As you can imagine, this was a disquieting prospect for the Keres family, as Keres was considered a collaborator for taking part in tournaments during the German occupation. Indeed Keres found it extremely difficult to restart his chess career, and it was only after representations to higher authorities and a few false starts that he was able to take part in the 15th Soviet Championship of 1947, which he won. I find it hard to imagine how you could ever focus on playing chess to any standard after living through something like that.

In the 1947 Soviet Championships, you also see Flohr – another player tipped for the World Champion's title in the late 1930s – driven to the Soviet Union by the circumstances of the war and finishing 7th-8th. And that's not even to mention talents like Rauzer, Riumin, A. and I. Rabinovich, Troitzky and L. Kubbel, who did not survive the war.

Running as a leitmotif throughout the book are Botvinnik's ever more desperate attempts to secure a match with Alekhine for the World Championship, a title that you feel both Botvinnik and his influential supporters felt was his right. I had gathered already from various sources how gladly Botvinnik wanted a match with the ageing Alekhine, but until I read Voronkov's narrative, I hadn't understood the extent

to which the spectre of a match influenced Botvinnik's choices and actions through those years. For example, the 1941 'Match Tournament for the title of Soviet Absolute Champion' was needed to 'correct' Bondarevsky's and Lilienthal's mistake of winning the 1940 Soviet Championship (Botvinnik finished in shared 5th place), as it was doubtful that Botvinnik could challenge Alekhine if he wasn't even the best player in Soviet Russia. But just think of the effect on Bondarevsky and Lilienthal when a great tournament win turns out to be worthless.

There are many amazing games I could show you, but I loved this win of Viacheslav Ragozin over David Bronstein in the 1945 Soviet Championship. Actually, another interesting leitmotif of the later stages of the book is the fairly grudging reactions of Bronstein's colleagues to his rise through the ranks! Bearing in mind that just four years after he finished 6th in the 1947 Soviet Championship, Bronstein was challenging Botvinnik for the World Championship, I have the feeling that some people were quite shocked by his progress!

**Viacheslav Ragozin
David Bronstein**
Moscow Soviet Championship
final 1945
Italian Game, Evans Gambit

1.e4 e5 2.♘f3 ♘c6 3.♗c4 ♗c5 4.b4 ♗xb4 5.c3 ♗a5 6.d4 d6 7.♕b3 ♘h6

'One look at this move is enough to make any sensible chess player

coil back in fright, but Bronstein, as we know, is certainly not a timid person', according to the tournament bulletin! This was actually the second time that Bronstein had played this move... and this game gave him his second loss! The engine certainly doesn't see it as the best move, but also not as the worst!

8.♗xh6 gxh6 9.♗xf7+ ♔f8

'I wasn't afraid of the exposed king and I played a few hundred games like this against [Semyon Abramovich] Sauskan' (an elderly Kiev player), according to Bronstein.

10.dxe5 ♕e7 11.♗d5 ♘xe5 12.♘xe5 ♕xe5 13.♕a3 ♗b6 14.♘d2 ♗c5

Just think of the effect on Bondarevsky and Lilienthal when a great tournament win turns out to be worthless

14...c6 15.♗b3 ♕c5 is an idea mentioned by Boleslavsky, who however recommended 16.♕b2 ♕xf2+ 17.♔d1 as the refutation, when Black's king and queen are caught on the newly-opened f-file. However, Marin points out the engine line 17...♕xg2 18.♖f1+ ♗f2 19.♔c2 ♔e7, when all is well and Black is winning!

15.♕b2 c6 16.♗b3 b5 17.0-0 ♔e7 18.♘f3 ♕g7 19.♔h1 ♗d7 20.e5

It doesn't actually look so bad for Black to me: there are plenty of open lines against the white kingside! However, the engine says +3 (and rising!) so the pressure along the f- and g-files is clearly illusory.

20...♖af8 21.exd6+ ♔xd6 22.♘d4 ♔c7 23.♖ad1 ♗d6 24.♖fe1 ♕g5 25.♗e6

A strong move swapping off one of Black's key pieces for defending his king and attacking the white kingside.

25...♖f6 26.♗xd7 ♔xd7 27.a4 a6 28.axb5 cxb5 29.♕a2 ♖a8 30.♘f3 ♕c5 31.♘e5+ ♔c7 32.♕a5+ ♔c8 33.♘d3 ♕h5 34.h3

34.♘f4 is a beautiful line pointed out by Marin, covering h2 while attacking the queen and uncovering the d-file! 34...♗xf4 35.♕d8+ ♔b7 36.♖d7+ ♔c6 37.♕xf6+ ♔xd7 38.♖e7+ mates.

34...♔b7 35.c4 ♖f3

A typically tricky Bronstein defence! **36.♘f4** Now it happens! This time the knight on f4 covers the h3-pawn! **36...♖xf4 37.♖xd6 ♕f7 38.♕b6+** 1-0.

All in all, a fantastic book! Most of us are going to be stuck inside for the next month with a new Covid lockdown – this is a perfect book to help you pass that time!

■ ■ ■

Caruana's Ruy Lopez – A White repertoire for Club Players by Fabiano Caruana (New In Chess) was a book that made me raise my eyebrows when I saw it: would Fabiano really have time to write an opening book? Then I read the blurb at the back, which said the book was based on Caruana's ChessBase video series *Navigating the Ruy Lopez*. Looking further inside, I read that this book is a transcription

Caruana's tone remains conversational, light and focused on general explanations throughout

of that 2019 video course. It seemed a little off the beaten track and it didn't grab me immediately so I only came back to the book a couple of months later. When I finally did sit down to read it, I really liked it!

First of all, the tone of the book is unusual. It's pretty much in the nature of a video course that you focus on general explanations and keep the complex variations to a minimum (they take so long to demonstrate!) Normally when you write a book however, the long variations creep in and the material inevitably gets more complex. Here the tone remains conversational, light and focused on general explanations throughout. It works particularly well because Caruana's understanding and experience is so good. The book is peppered with references to his own games, and his feelings about particular lines. He also explains the logic of the opening beautifully: why he is making choices

Caruana's Ruy Lopez
Fabiano Caruana
New In Chess, 2021
★★★★☆

at move 7 or 8, what he is trying to avoid and what his experience has taught him. My experience of Ruy Lopez positions is quite uneven – I've analysed plenty of different systems at times but never had a really complete 1.e4 e5 Ruy Lopez repertory – and I felt that Caruana's explanations were knitting it all together, filling in lots of logic gaps and explaining to me the real reasons I'd chosen my systems! I used it a lot during the Nepomniachtchi-Carlsen match as Ian tried to squeeze out edges with his Anti-Marshalls. The unusual systems Magnus went for are not in the book, but the logic of what he did is, and I found that extremely useful background information. I would unreservedly recommend this to any player wanting to start out with 1.e4 and looking for a good Ruy Lopez repertory after 1...e5 2.♘f3 ♘c6 3.♗b5. 4 stars!

■ ■ ■

We move on now to *The Scandinavian for Club Players* by Thomas Willemze (New In Chess), which features the longest book subtitle I've ever seen: 'Start playing an unsidesteppable & low maintenance response to 1.e4 and simultaneously improve your chess technique'!

In all fairness I'm not a big fan of the Scandinavian. I remember picking up the 3...♕d6 Scandinavian briefly in 2016, having been inspired by writing about Sergey Tiviakov's successes in *Chess for Life* and finding out that the middlegame positions (with black pawns on e6 and c6 against a white pawn on d4) just didn't appeal to me. So I opened Thomas Willemze's book

**The Scandinavian
for Club Players
Thomas Willemze
New In Chess, 2021**
★★★★☆

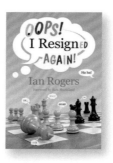

**Oops I resigned
again
Ian Rogers
Russell Enterprises,
2021**
★★★☆☆

on the 3...♛a5 Scandinavian with a slightly sour expression, expecting to be confronted with series of diagrams of my least favourite pawn structure!

However, it wasn't that bad in the end – actually it was pretty good! Willemze has clearly given a lot of thought to organizing the book for the benefit of his audience and it works really well. Willemze manages to organize the material both theoretically and thematically.

For example, Chapter 1 deals with the line:

1.e4 d5 2.exd5 ♛xd5 3.♘c3 ♛a5 4.d4 ♘f6 5.♘f3 ♝f5 6.♝c4

with the chapter title '6.♝c4 – the d4-d5 break', explaining the specific theory of 6.♝c4, White's typical and dangerous idea of breaking with

Willemze has clearly given a lot of thought to organizing the book for the benefit of his audience

d4-d5 and Black's ways of dealing with it.

The chapter is divided into short sections with game examples of White and Black successes, then specific theoretical sections (brief but covering the essentials) before a final Flash Card page to reinforce the lessons. Subsequent chapters are organized in a similar fashion: '6.♘e5 – kingside expansion' (dealing with the common White plan of throwing g- and h-pawns forward to chase the light-squared bishop) and '6.♝d2 – aggressive queenside castling'. Some exercises at the end of each section round off the learning experience. It's a really efficient way of learning both the opening theory and some of your opponent's general plans at the same time!

The opening recommendations themselves are pretty good: easy to pick up without too much memory strain and pretty solid! It's basically a really good coaching effort and definitely recommended for any club players looking for an easy response to 1.e4 with some good chess instruction thrown in! 4 stars!

■ ■ ■

We round off with a book that makes you run to the index at the back to check for your name (well its absence actually!) before you can relax and start enjoying it! I'm talking about *Oops I resigned again* by Ian Rogers (Russell Enterprises), adorned with a lovely foreword by a player responsible for one of the more famous erroneous resignations of recent times, 2018 US Champion Sam Shankland.

Rogers brings together 100 examples of premature resignations for our

enjoyment! What surprised me most of all was how plausible many of these resignations were – I could easily imagine myself resigning a few of these games myself! I'll just give one example which cost me a few minutes to work out before I managed to get past Black's impressive concept and understand why White all the same shouldn't resign!

**Jacek Flis (2345)
Aleksandr Poluljahov (2515)**
Katowice 1993

50...♝c8 was a very sneaky idea from Black. After **51.♔d2 ♖xd3+** Now after 52.♔xd3 ♔g6, White cannot prevent the black king from snaffling the rook with ...♔g5. Very ingenious, don't you think? White thought so too and resigned! However, there is a fly in the ointment...
53.♔c4 ♔g5 54.♖xh6 ♔xh6 55.♔d5

draws as White captures the e5-pawn leaving Black with the wrong-coloured rook's pawn for his bishop!

A pretty fun slim book of 160 pages, perfect for a bit of daily tactical training! 3 stars! ■

Jan Timman

Euwe to the Max

Max Euwe (1901-1981) is one of the 'lesser known' World Champions. In part because there is no representative games collection of the Dutchman. **JAN TIMMAN** is remedying this gap in chess literature and argues that Euwe not only held the world title from 1935 to 1937, but that at his peak his countryman was also the strongest player in the world.

I have been working on a book of Max Euwe's best games for a while. I had planned the project years ago, mainly to honour the only Dutchman ever to become chess World Champion. But I had a secondary motive: there is no representative Euwe games book in existence. *From My Chess Games* contains 75 games from the 1920-1937 period. *Max Euwe. The Biography* contains 116 games from his entire career, but quite a few of them have little or no commentary. In addition, that selection is not representative of his best games, because it includes too many defeats and draws. Then there's one more book, which has only appeared in Dutch: *Keuze uit zijn beste partijen* (A selection of his best games). It contains a curious selection of 47 games, many of them from the 1950-1953 period, when Euwe was far from his peak. I suspect that the compilers of the book had just raked together Euwe's comments from the federation journal of that time.

According to *Chessmetrics*, Euwe was truly the strongest player in the world for over a year during the time he won the World Championship. He was a late bloomer in this respect, having only reached his highest level after turning 30. But a decade earlier, he had already beaten several top players from an earlier generation several times: Tarrasch, Maroczy, Rubinstein, Bogoljubow and Réti. And Euwe always evinced an excellent sense for the initiative and sharp calculating powers. Many of his wins feel like contemporary games.

With Geza Maroczy, 31 years his senior, he had a special connection. According to *Chessmetrics*, the Hungarian was the world's strongest player between 1904 and 1907. In 1906

he was to play a World Championship match against Lasker in Vienna, but it never took place, even though the preparations already were at an advanced stage. In 1919, a Communist revolution took place in Hungary, forcing Maroczy to flee. He ended up in the Netherlands, which hadn't suffered from the post-World War I financial mess, since our country had stayed neutral. This is how Maroczy became the 18-year-old Euwe's teacher. Their cooperation lasted till the 1935 World Championship match, during which Maroczy acted as Euwe's second. In 1921, they played a 12-game match, in which Euwe was leading 4-2 halfway. Game 6 in particular was very good, and highlights the sharpness of Euwe's calculating powers. Remarkably enough, this game does not feature in *From My Chess Games*.

Max Euwe
Geza Maroczy
Bad Aussee match 1921 (6)
French Defence, MacCutcheon Variation
1.e4 e6 2.d4 d5 3.♘c3 ♘f6 4.♗g5 ♗b4

The MacCutcheon Variation, which was fairly common in that time.
5.e5 h6 6.♗d2 ♗xc3 7.bxc3 ♘e4

8.♕g4 g6

9.h4 Euwe is fighting Maroczy with his own weapons! The text had been introduced in Maroczy-Spielmann, Berlin 1920. The main aim of the advance is to deploy the rook via h3. This is still played, but usually in the move order 9.♗d3 ♘xd2 10.♔xd2 c5 11.h4. There's no real difference, since both players' moves are virtually forced.

9...c5 10.♗d3 ♘xd2 11.♔xd2

11...♕a5

Spielmann decided to close the position with 11...c4 here. The drawback of this strategy is that Black will find it next to impossible to create counterplay on the queenside and in the centre, so that White ends up with a free hand on the kingside. The alternative 11...♘c6 is more common these days, but in some cases it leads to a transposition.

Euwe was truly the strongest player in the world for over a year during the time he won the world championship

For 20-year-old Max Euwe, drawing a 12-game match against Geza Maroczy was a notable achievement. Between 1904 and 1907 the Hungarian had been the strongest player in the world.

12.♖h3

Consistent; but many years later, Peter Leko played 12.♘f3 here, intending to recapture on d4 with the knight. This yields White a slight strategic plus.

12...cxd4

In Spoelman-Glek, Hoogeveen 2003, Black played 12...♘c6, the point being that Black will control square f3 after 13.♗xg6 ♘xd4, preventing a decisive attack by White. The game continued 14.♔d1 ♖g8 15.♗xf7+ ♔xf7 16.♕h5+ ♔e7 17.cxd4 ♖xg2 18.♘e2

♗d7, and now White could have preserved the balance with 19.♕f3 (instead of 19.♕xh6) 19...♖ag8 20.♖g3.

13.♗xg6! Of course. Play is getting ultra-sharp now.

13...♕c7

It's generally inadvisable to go for a passive move in such a sharp position. I think Maroczy had a deeply calculated variation in mind here, which was almost miraculously refuted.

Earlier that year Euwe had also gotten the position after 13.♗xg6. In Euwe-Te Kolsté, Nijmegen 1921, there followed 13...dxc3+, which is clearly stronger. White now has a choice between two king moves:

– Euwe played 14.♔d1, which was later repeated in some lesser-known games. With 14...♖f8! (instead of Te

Kolsté's 14...♕c7) Black could have got an advantage. A possible continuation is: 15.♖f3 ♕c5 16.♗h5 ♘c6, and the situation is not easy for White.

– 14.♔e1! ♖f8 15.♖f3 ♕c5 16.♗h5 ♘c6 17.♕g7, and now we see why the king had to go to e1: Black has no check on d4. After 17...♕e7 18.♘e2 ♗d7, incidentally, he has nothing to fear. The position is equal.

The alternative 13...♖f8, to solidly cover the f-pawn, was also playable. After 14.♖f3 dxc3+ (or 14...♕c5) the chances are roughly equal.

14.♖f3

14...♖g8

Black wants to preserve the option of taking with the queen on c3 later, a theme that can also surface in the Winawer Variation of the French. After 14...dxc3+ 15.♔d1 Black doesn't have a good defence, e.g. 15...♖g8 16.♖xf7 ♖xg6 17.♖xc7 ♖xg4 18.♖xc8+ ♔d7 19.♖h8, and the pin on the back rank will eventually spell disaster for Black.

15.♖xf7 ♕xc3+

16.♔e2!

The correct king move. In A. Horvath-Huang, Budapest 1998, there followed 16.♔d1? ♕xa1+ 17.♔e2 ♘d8, and White had insufficient compensation for the sacrificed material.

16...d3+

This must be what Maroczy had set his sights on. The situation looks very promising for Black – but White has a narrow route to a large advantage.

17.cxd3 ♕xe5+ 18.♔f3!

Euwe has spotted sharply that he'll be able to run away from the queen checks in this way.

18...♖f8

Maroczy is unaware of the danger. The text is refuted beautifully. A better defence was 18...♘c6, after which White coolly continues with 19.g3 to vacate square g2 for his king. Black now has the following possibilities:

– 19...♖f8 20.♖xf8+ ♔xf8 21.♖b1 b6 22.♔g2, with a large advantage for White.

– 19...♕d4 20.♖f4+ ♔e7 21.♖e1! ♕e5 22.♖f7+ ♔d6 23.♖c1 ♖g7 24.♖f8!, and White has a winning advan-

tage. The black king remains in great danger.

– Probably best is 19...♖xg6. After 20.♕xg6 ♘e7 21.♖xe7+ ♔xe7 22.♖c1 ♕f6+ 23.♕xf6+ ♔xf6 24.♘e2 e5 25.d4 Black has the unlikely computer move 25...♗h3!, preserving his drawing chances. It's easy to show, incidentally, that the bishop should be taken to h3; it would be vulnerable on any other square.

19.♖f5+!! The fantastic point of the previous move. Study-like motifs are playing a major part here. It is important that Black cannot continue to protect his king's knight.

19...♔d7 After 19...♔e7 20.♕b4+ Black also loses quickly.

20.♖xf8 ♕xa1 21.♖f7+ ♔d8 22.♕b4 ♘d7 23.♕d6 ♕h8 24.♘e2 e5

25.♘f4 Elegantly rounding off the proceedings. But with 25.♘c3 White would have been able to force a checkmate more quickly. The computer announces mate in 7.

When regarding this position as a chess problem, it is interesting to see how exactly it works: 25...e4+ 26.♔g4 ♕e8

ANALYSIS DIAGRAM

and now the typical problem move 27.♔h3! (since 27.♘xd5 can still be met by 27...♕e6+ 28.♕xe6 ♘e5+). Then it continues as follows: 27...♕e6+ 28.♕xe6 ♘b6 29.♖f8+ ♔c7 30.♘b5+ ♔b8, and now an unpinning move like 31.♗f5, and the queen can deliver mate.

25...exf4 26.♗f5 ♕e8 27.♗xd7 ♗xd7 28.♖f8 Black resigned.

Maroczy managed to even the score in the end, but the result was still a great success for the 20-year-old.

A sharp battle, full of ideas

The tournament in Mährisch Ostrau – present-day Ostrava in the Czech Republic – in 1923 was a great triumph for Lasker, who left his rivals far behind with 10 out of 13. Euwe scored his first modest success in the international tournament scene, finishing shared fifth with seven points and managing to beat Rubinstein for the first time in the process.

I remember my trainer Hans Bouwmeester showing me the game in 1967, and that it fascinated me; such a sharp battle, full of ideas, and also so solid-looking strategically. The computer gave new insights, of course. At one point, Rubinstein had had an excellent, virtually winning position. I briefly hesitated about including the game in the book – but there were enough reasons to appreciate Euwe's merits in the fight. He set up an excellent attack, avoided a draw despite a setback, and struck brilliantly when Rubinstein dropped

the ball. Moreover, the middlegame fight is exceptionally interesting and instructive.

Max Euwe
Akiba Rubinstein
Mährisch Ostrau 1923
Queen's Pawn Opening, Colle System

1.♘f3 d5 2.d4 ♘f6 3.e3 e6 4.♗d3 c5 5.b3

Euwe goes for a system that Artur Jussupow used to like playing later.

5...♘c6 6.0-0 ♗d6 7.♗b2 0-0 8.a3 A typical move in this system. White prevents a possible knight sortie to b4.

8...b6 9.♘e5 ♗b7 10.♘d2 ♕e7

An unfortunate move, since it's better to keep square e7 for the queen's knight. Good alternatives are 10...♕c7 and 10...♖c8.

10...♘e7 is also possible, while Rubinstein decided to go for the curious 10...a6 against Walter John in Ostend 1907. Even that move isn't bad, since Black is preparing ...b6-b5.

11.f4!

'An important reinforcement of the

white position,' Euwe observes. It is also the sign for the attack. White can now deploy his king's rook in the attack via square f3.

11...♖fd8 12.♖f3

Consistent; but the alternative 12.♕f3 was stronger. It is very important to keep a firm grip on square e4. Black will find it hard to come up with a good defensive plan.

12...♘e4

The correct idea, but the wrong execution. Correct was 12...cxd4! first. It is important to resolve the tension in the centre before anything else. Wit has two options:

– 13.exd4 ♘e4 14.♘xe4 (14.♖h3 is met by 14...f5) 14...dxe4 15.♗xe4 ♘xe5 16.♗xh7+! ♔xh7 17.♖h3+ ♔g8 18.fxe5 ♗xe5 19.♕h5 f5 20.dxe5 ♕c5+ 21.♔h1 ♖d2 22.♕h7+ ♔f7 23.♕h5+, with a draw.

– 13.♖h3 h6! (a good preventive measure, since 13...dxe3 14.♗xh7+ ♘xh7 15.♕h5 is dangerous for Black) 14.exd4 ♘e4 15.♕e2 f5 16.♘df3, and the position is equal.

13.♖h3 Entirely according to plan; but 13.dxc5 was also possible. After 13...bxc5 14.♗xe4 dxe4 15.♖g3 f6 16.♘ec4 ♗c7 17.♕h5 White is better.

Max Euwe was fond of flying, not a passion that people automatically associated with 'the professor'.

13...f5

It was too late for 13...cxd4 already, because White is not forced to recapture the pawn. 14.♗xe4 dxe4 15.♕h5 h6 16.♖g3 yields him a strong attack. Black has the following defensive options:

– 16...♗xe5 17.fxe5 ♔h7 18.♘xe4 g6 19.♕e2 ♘xe5 20.exd4 ♗xe4 21.♕xe4 ♘d7 22.♖e1, with a large advantage for White.

– 16...♗xe5 17.fxe5 ♗c7 (17...♗c5 is met decisively by 18.b4 dxe3 19.♘b3!, winning a piece) 18.♗xd4 ♔h7 19.♖f1, and White gets a decisive attack.

– After 16...f5 White has a number of measured moves that will yield him a critical advantage. The main line goes as follows: 17.♘xc6 ♗xc6 18.♘c4! ♗c7 19.♖d1! b5 20.♖xd4 bxc4 21.♖xd8+ ♖xd8 22.♗xg7 ♕xg7 23.♕xh6!, and wins.

14.♗xe4

The immediate 14.♕h5 would have been more accurate. Black can defend in two ways:

– 14...♘f6 (the best) 15.♕h4 cxd4 16.♘xc6 (the sharp 16.♘df3 is also possible) 16...♗xc6 17.♗xd4, with a large advantage for White.

– 14...h6 15.♗xe4 dxe4 16.♘xc6 ♗xc6 17.♖g3 cxd4, and now White wins exactly as shown in the third line in the above comment, starting with 18.♘c4. At every turn, we see how important the timely insertion of the swap on d4 was for Black. When the long diagonal is opened for the white queen's bishop, White will get a promising attack.

14...dxe4 15.♕h5

15...♗xe5!

This is the difference. Now that White has swapped on e4, Black can allow the capture on h7.

16.♕xh7+ ♔f7

17.fxe5

Euwe lets this move pass without comment, so we don't know if he was knowingly playing for a win. I think he was: it's not difficult to see that White can force a draw with 17.dxe5. In this situation, the transaction of swapping two rooks for the queen, as in the game, is not correct. With a fixed pawn structure and an open d-file, the rooks would be far stronger than the queen. This means that 17...♖xd2 is the only option, after which White forces a perpetual with 18.♕h5+. This was absolutely the objectively best way for White to play, because the text leaves him in a dubious position.

17...♖h8 The point of the previous move. Rubinstein forces the swap of two rooks against the queen in very favourable conditions.

18.♕xh8 ♖xh8 19.♖xh8

19...♗a6

A good strategic move, but 19...cxd4 would have been stronger. The variations were hard to calculate, however. After 20.exd4 Black has two moves: – 20...♕g5 21.♘c4 ♗a6 22.♗c1 ♕g4 23.♘d6+ ♔e7 24.♗e3 f4 25.c4! fxe3 26.♖f1, and Black won't find it easy to convert his material plus.

ANALYSIS DIAGRAM

A possible continuation is: 26...♘d8 27.h3 ♕g6 28.♖ff8 e2 29.♔f2 e1♕+ 30.♔xe1 ♕g3+ 31.♔f1 ♕d3+ 32.♔g1 ♕xd4+ 33.♔f1 ♕a1+ 34.♔e2 ♕b2+ 35.♔e3 ♕c1+ 36.♔xe4 ♗b7+ 37.♔d3 ♕d1+ 38.♔c3 ♕e1+ 39.♔d3 ♗e4+ 40.♘xe4 ♘f7, and White has to give his rook for the knight. But even then, the win remains problematic for Black.
– 20...♘xe5 21.dxe5 ♕c5+ 22.♔h1 ♕xc2 23.♘c4 e3 24.♖g1 e2 25.♖e1 (after 25.♘d6+ ♔e7 26.♘xb7 ♕xb2 27.♖c8 ♕xe5 White will be hopelessly lost; the knight no longer counts) 25...♔g6 (threatening 26...♕e4) 26.♖h3!, and White has some chances of survival.

20.♘f1

Too passive. With the knight sacrifice 20.♘xe4! White would just about have managed to preserve the balance. The spectacular main line continues as follows: 20...fxe4 21.c4 ♕g5 22.♖f1+ ♔e7 23.♗c1 cxd4 24.a4! ♘xe5 25.exd4 ♘f3+ 26.♔h1 ♕g6 27.♗e3 ♗b7

and now 28.♖h3! is the saving move. White is in no hurry to take the knight – which has nowhere to go anyway. Black will be unable to make progress here.

20...♕d7

Again, 20...cxd4 would have been strong here. After 21.exd4 ♘xe5! 22.dxe5 ♕c5+ 23.♔h1 ♕xc2 24.♗d4

♗xf1 25.♖xf1 ♕d3 Black wins back the piece, and will get a powerful pawn majority.

20...♗xf1 21.♖xf1 ♕g5, as indicated by Euwe, would also have yielded Black a large advantage. There could follow: 22.♗c1 cxd4 23.exd4 ♕g4 24.c3 ♕e2!, and Black is holding all the strategic trumps.

And finally, the immediate 20...♕g5 would also have been possible. White is in trouble, as witness 21.c4 cxd4 22.♗xd4 ♘xd4 23.exd4 e3 24.♖e1 ♕f4 25.♘xe3 ♕xd4 26.♖h3 ♕xe5, and, here, too, the black queen dominates.

21.♖d1

21...♘xe5 A serious mistake. Black should have inserted the swap on f1. After 21...♗xf1 22.♔xf1 cxd4 23.♗xd4 ♘xe5 Black is still better, but with 24.♔e1! White can limit the damage. Black cannot prevent the minor piece swap, after which White should be able to hold.

22.d5! A magnificent breakthrough. White is suddenly winning. His pieces are coordinating perfectly.

22...♘g4 What else? 22...♘g6 would have run into the devastating

23.♖d8!. After 23...♕xd8 24.dxe6+ ♔e7 25.♖xd8 ♔xd8 26.♘g3 Black's position is hopeless.

23.dxe6+ ♕xe6 24.♖hd8 ♗b5 25.c4 ♗e8 26.♖1d5

More accurate was 26.h3, leaving Black on the ropes.

26...f4 Black's best practical chance was 26...♗c6 27.♖5d6 ♕e7, when White is still winning but has to play accurately. The correct move after 28.h3 ♘h6 is 29.♗e5!. There could follow: 29...♕xe5 30.♖xc6 f4 31.♖d7+

♔g8 32.exf4 ♕xf4 33.♖e6, with a technically winning position.

The text appears to generate some counterplay, but Euwe is at his best now.

27.h3 This pawn move required sharp calculation.

27...fxe3 28.♘g3!

The point of the previous move. But Black hasn't quite run out of resources yet.

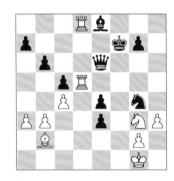

28...e2 29.♘xe2 ♘e3 30.♖g5 g6 31.♘f4 ♕e7

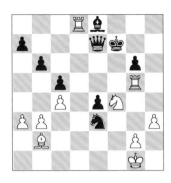

32.♖xg6! The elegant death blow. Black cannot take the rook on d8 in view of mate in two.

32...♘f5 33.♖f6+ ♔g8 34.♖xe8+ ♕xe8 35.♖xf5 e3 36.♖e5

Black resigned.

Sacrifices on empty squares

Ray Keene has pointed out that Euwe had a specialty: sacrificing pieces on empty squares. His wins over Alekhine in Zurich 1934 and Geller in Zurich 1953 are famous examples. During the selection process, I stumbled on a new

one, from a match against six-time Belgian champion Edgar Colle. Euwe played two matches against Colle, in 1924 and in 1928, winning both with unequivocal scores.

Max Euwe
Edgar Colle
Amsterdam 1928 (3rd match game)

position after 15...♞c6

White has come out of the opening (a Nimzo-Indian) with a plus. He's going to launch an attack.

16.f4 As in the game against Rubinstein, the correct approach. White supports his strongly positioned knight.

16...f6 17.♞g6
Penetrating the enemy lines.

17...♖f7 A more natural reaction was 17...♖fe8.

18.♗b1

A promising plan: Euwe is going to set up a battery on the b1-h7 diagonal. The computer prefers 18.♕d1, with a large advantage, but the text makes greater demands of Black.

18...♞e7 His best bet was probably 18...♖c7, preparing for White's plan.

Edgar Colle, the gifted Belgian master who tragically died at the young age of 34, lost two matches against Max Euwe.

19.♕c2 ♕e6
And here, Black's only defence was 19...♞xg6 20.♕xg6 ♔f8, even though his situation after 21.♕h7 would be highly awkward. The unsuspecting text runs into a resounding surprise.

20.♞h8!! What a joy it must be to play such a move. White wins.
20... ♕xe3+ 21.♔h1 cxd4 22.♕h7+ ♔f8 23.♗g6 ♞xg6 24.♞xg6+ ♔e8 25.♕g8+ Black resigned.

Last major success

Euwe's last great success was the Staunton tournament in Groningen 1946, where he finished second, half a point behind Mikhail Botvinnik, and one-and-a-half points ahead of Vasily Smyslov. In the first round,

he won a famous endgame against Daniel Yanofsky, in which I have unearthed several important new finesses.

Max Euwe
Daniel Yanofsky
Groningen 1946

position after 25...♔f7

Euwe has liquidated to this bishop ending, which is unwinnable because of the opposite-coloured bishops – despite his extra pawn. But there are traps for Black.

26.a4 ♗b3 27.a5 ♗c2
A careless move that allows White to introduce an elegant, study-like turn. With 27...c5 or 27...♗c4 Black could have ensured the draw without any problems to speak of.

28.♗c5!!

'A little trifle,' Euwe calls this fantastic move in his comment. Here you see an example of the modesty that was so characteristic of Euwe. The bishop move has gone down in history.

28...♗d3

The only move. The a-pawn had to be stopped.

29.♗xd6 ♗xe4 30.a6 c5 31.♗xc5

31...h5!

Both Euwe and Kasparov – in *My Great Predecessors*, Part II – give this advance an '!'. It is part of a plan in which Black can build an unassailable defence.

32.♔f2 ♗d3

Another '!' from Euwe and Kasparov – and it's true that the text fits in the plan to throw up an unassailable fortress. It looks as follows: Black forces the a-pawn to a7, and then plays his bishop to the long diagonal. After blocking the connected passed pawns Black can maintain a defensive line: if the white king goes to the queenside via the g1-a7 diagonal, the black king will shadow it along the h3-c8 diagonal.

In reality, however, the text is a serious error. There was a different priority: centralizing the king to prevent the white king to penetrate decisively.

Only 32...♔e6! would have allowed Black to survive by the skin of his teeth. The main line goes as follows: 33.g4 hxg4 34.♔e3 ♗c6! (the only square for the bishop) 35.♔f4 ♔d7 36.♔xg4 ♔c7 37.♔f5 ♔e8! 38.♗d4 g6+ 39.♔f6 ♗b8, and White cannot win. Black will not get into zugzwang, because his king will always have a square to move to. It is interesting to see how the black king and bishop switch jobs in this line.

33.a7 ♗e4 34.g3

An automatic move that lacks energy.

With the surprising 34.g4!! White could have won in study-like fashion, the main idea behind the pawn sac being that White is taking away square f5 from the black king (for the moment). The loss of the white g-pawn is of little consequence, since he keeps the h-pawn, which will eventually decide the issue. There could follow: 34...hxg4 35.♔g3 ♗f3 36.♔f4 ♔e6 37.♔d4 g6 38.♔g5 ♔f7 39.b4, and the win plays itself, as it will later in the game.

34...♔e6 35.♔e3 ♗g2

And in this way Yanofsky neglects the defensive line he could have maintained with 35...♔f5. After 36.h3 ♗g2 37.♔d4 ♔e6 White will be unable to make progress.

36.♔f4!

Bursting through the defensive line.

36...g6 37.g4 hxg4 38.♔xg4 ♗h1 39.♔g5 ♔f7 40.♗d4 ♗g2 41.h4 ♗h1 42.b4 ♗g2 43.b5 ♗h1 44.♗f6 ♗g2

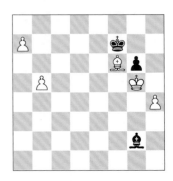

45.h5! The decisive breakthrough that presents the white king with free passage to the queenside.

45...gxh5 46.♔f5

Black resigned. ∎

John Donaldson

CURRENT ELO: **2417**

DATE OF BIRTH: **September 24, 1958**

PLACE OF BIRTH: **Los Angeles, California**

PLACE OF RESIDENCE: **Berkeley, California**

What is your favourite city?
New York City for its energy and San Francisco for its beauty.

What was the last great meal you had?
It's been too long! Now I look forward to starting the day with a bowl of oatmeal with blueberries, walnuts, chia seeds, cinnamon and a pinch of cardamon.

What drink brings a smile to your face?
Genmaicha green tea.

Which book would you give to a friend?
Anything written by the late Philip Kerr, particularly his *Bernie Gunther* series.

What book are you currently reading?
The Dark Hours by Michael Connelly.

What is your all-time favourite movie?
I love film noir, especially set in Los Angeles, so I will go with *Double Indemnity*, *Sunset Boulevard* and *Chinatown*.

What music do you listen to?
Albums from the late 1960s from bands based in San Francisco – Jefferson Airplane, Santana, Sly and the Family Stone, Grateful Dead, Quicksilver Messenger Service, and the list goes on.

Is there a work of art that moves you?
Ugolino and His Sons by Carpeaux.

What is your earliest chess memory?
A visit to the Tacoma Chess Club shortly after the Fischer-Spassky match. It was incredibly smoky, which was normal for the time. After the first night I was hooked for life.

Who is your favourite chess player?
Bobby Fischer, because he was far ahead

of his contemporaries and did it by himself without a team.

Is there a chess book that had a profound influence on you?
My 60 Memorable Games, *Think Like A Grandmaster* and *How to Open a Chess Game*. That said, I would say 90 percent of the best chess books ever written were published in the last twenty years.

What was your best result ever?
Two GM norms in 2002 and 2003, although I remember a half point miss at Vancouver 2000 much better!

And the best game you played?
Maybe Donaldson-Kudrin, 2003 US Championship.

What was the most exciting chess game you ever saw?
Fomenko-Radchenko, USSR 1967.

What is your favourite square?
f3 for ♘f3, my favourite opening move.

What are chess players particularly good at (except for chess)?
Languages and adapting to new technology (myself the exception on both counts).

Facebook, Instagram, Snapchat, or?
I'm not interested in social media, but do have favourite websites and magazines including *Chessdryad.com* and *Northwest Chess*.

Which three people would you like to invite for dinner?
Bobby Fischer, Boris Spassky and Mikhail Tal in the mid to late 1960s before Bobby's demons got to him.

What is your life motto?
FIDE's motto, *Gens Una Sumus*, is a good one.

Who or what would you like to be if you weren't yourself?
A detective or a dog walker.

What is the best piece of advice you were ever given?
GM Peter Biyiasas advised me one should only take a job outside of chess if it pays twice as much (he found one!).

Is there something you'd love to learn?
Languages and how to type really fast.

What would people be surprised to know about you?
I have been a vegetarian, later vegan since 1976, prefer to travel by train and am a passionate track and field fan.

What is your greatest fear?
That climate change will not be adequately addressed until it's too late.

And your greatest regret?
I still think about the finishes of the 1986 Olympiad and the 1997 World Team Championship. In both cases the US teams played exceptionally well, but fell just short of winning. Could we have done things a little differently?

Is a knowledge of chess useful in everyday life?
Chess requires one to think logically, a skill that is useful in a world in which there is so much fake news.

What does it mean to be a chess player?
You speak a universal language and don't need to find a hobby when you retire.